GABE & IZZY

STANDING UP FOR AMERICA'S BULLIED

Facing page: Gabe with students from Lake Fenton
Torrey Hill Elementary School

GABE & IZZY

STANDING UP FOR AMERICA'S BULLIED

GABRIELLE FORD with SARAH THOMSON

DIAL BOOKS
An Imprint of Penguin Group (USA)

DIAL BOOKS FOR YOUNG READERS
Published by the Penguin Group
Penguin Group (USA) LLC
375 Hudson Street
New York, New York 10014

USA * Canada * UK * Ireland * Australia
New Zealand * India * South Africa * China

penguin.com
A Penguin Random House Company

Published simultaneously in the United States of America by
Dial Books for Young Readers and Puffin Books,
imprints of Penguin Young Readers Group, 2014

CIP data is available

Dial Books ISBN 978-0-8037-4062-4

Printed in the United States of America

1 3 5 7 9 10 8 6 4 2

First and foremost, I dedicate this book to my coonhound Izzy, my best friend evermore, the center of my universe. Her long, velvety ears were often the first things to catch my tears. Without Izzy, I would not have discovered my inner gift for connecting with students, which helped me become a nationally renowned focal point for educators—a face, a voice for America's bullied.

Second, this book is sincerely dedicated to those who have suffered bullying at the hands of their classmates, to the students who have stood by not knowing what to do, and to those who bully.

Furthermore, this book is dedicated to all the students who have attended my school assemblies or events and have spoken with me afterward, shook my hand, hugged me, thanked me, gave me a high five, laughed with me, confided in me, danced for me, cried with me, rubbed Izzy's belly, patted her head, took photographs or shared their personal story, and wrote letters to me or posted comments on my online guest book. You asked me to continue spreading my story not only across the U.S. but all over the world! Your wish has come true. You moved me to write the words within this book after listening to you and reading your letters. Yes, I've read thousands of them, every one! THIS BOOK IS FOR YOU!

I'm just Gabe, grounded, given an unexpected and extraordinary story. But I am your voice! I have no doubt that this book will help you, and other students, for countless years to come.

Last but not least, I dedicate my book to my mom, who never gave up on me! She taught me the importance of forgiving others so that I would not hold on to hurt, anger, and bitterness or remain an unhappy person. My mom taught me that no one is perfect, and that every day is a new day for each of us, an opportunity to become a better person.

Mom, Izzy, and I spent many years traveling across the country, in and out of airports. She drove Izzy and me long distances through snowstorms, icy road conditions, rain, wind, and winding mountain roads, to ensure that we would be able to share our anti-bullying message.

When traveling by plane, Mom would pull Izzy in her wagon with one hand and push me in my wheelchair with the other. She would have to disassemble my wheelchair and Izzy's wagon every time we got on a plane, and reassemble them when we got off. After all that, she was still responsible for getting us from the airport to our destination!

I'm not sure how she did it all, but she did. She says bullying hurts not only the person being bullied but the family, too. She is passionate about bullying; she does not want anyone to feel its wrath, because she, too, experienced bullying first-hand as a young girl.

Years later, my stepfather, Rick, shared the driving with my mom. Both of them helped Izzy and me make our voices heard in a world of bullied students. No longer do students need to suffer in silence. I heard their cry, I am their voice!

Dear Reader,

I never imagined I would become a voice for the bullied. I never even imagined I would be bullied. But fate works in strange ways. When I was a girl, I dreamed of becoming a professional dancer. Dance was my first love. I danced tap, jazz, and ballet for years. I was pursuing my dream. Then, surprisingly, at about the age of thirteen, I began to lose my balance. I would fall and stumble. My family discovered I had a progressive, life-threatening disease called Friedreich's ataxia. I learned I wouldn't dance again, and someday I wouldn't be able to walk. I was heartbroken. My life would be a long fight. It was a new life I did NOT want.

I became different. I was bullied.

The bullying I endured hurt me deeply. For years, I would hide from classmates who teased me about the way I walked or pushed me into the lockers in the hall. I had speech class waived in high school because other students made fun of my voice. I began to spend long periods of time alone in my room at home. Just the thought of going into my school was pure torment. I didn't want to go out of the house, let alone to school!

And then a long-eared coonhound named Izzy

came into my life, and everything changed. In this book, you'll learn about my remarkable bond with Izzy: how she developed a mysterious condition similar to mine; how caring for her forced me out of hiding and launched me on the path to my life's purpose—becoming a speaker for the bullied.

Izzy and I became two of a kind, and through our shared experience I learned that while we don't always have a choice about what happens to us in life, we do always have a choice about how we treat those around us. I realize I am not the only one who has been bullied, nor am I the only one who has a life-threatening disease, but I am the only one with an Izzy dog!

Together, my beloved Izzy and I began to tour schools, speaking to students and educators about how to prevent bullying. I knew that fewer bullied students meant fewer broken people who would feel the pain, shame, and embarrassment I felt. I knew that together Izzy and I could make a difference.

As our story gained media attention, Izzy and I took it on the road, speaking to larger audiences all across the country. Our story has captivated hundreds of thousands of people, and it will captivate you, too.

This book is for you if you've been bullied, if you've been someone who bullies, if you've witnessed it or overheard it, or if you're just a dog lover like me who enjoys a good story! I can't tell you how many times I have felt alone, but I am here to tell you that you are not. I want you to know that if I can get through bullying, anyone can, and I hope you'll find strength in my story, as many students and educators have.

By accepting what has happened in my life, my purpose in life found me. I now embrace my sufferings and would not change my life. My dog, Izzy, really does have a voice, and together we have been given an amazing story, an incredible journey, and many students have stopped bullying one another when they read or hear about it. Knowing that sharing my experiences has prevented so many students from being bullied has been meaningful to me. I've come to learn that:

To the world you may be just one person, but to one person you may be the world.

I'd like to share a message from a student that has meant so much.

Dear Gabe,

You recently visited my high school, Tanque Verde. Your story basically saved my life. Early this week, I was thinking of ending my life. Not due to bullying but because of other reasons. You showed me that life is what you make it and that it can/will get better. You have given me such a hope and a will to see my bright future. Thank you so much for speaking to us and may you continue spreading your inspiration across the U.S., across the world. You are a true hero.

I will continue my purpose with determination. It's a passion that burns inside me.

I hope you will read and cherish my book. I hope you will read it to your children in the years to come. From speaking in schools and other venues, I know that my story appeals to all generations and leaves people inspired, motivated, and encouraged. We need this in a world of bullying. My wish for Izzy to live forever can come true because of you. This book will continue our work and help end bullying long after Izzy and I are gone.

I hope you will read my book and learn that not only can one person be the world to someone, but a dog can be, too. Izzy became the world to me and changed my life, and the lives of many others, forever. After you read my book I hope you will join Izzy and me and STAND AGAINST BULLYING. I hope you take the Gabe & Izzy Anti-Bullying Pledge. If you do, you will help Izzy and me make the world a better place.

Love, Gabe, and forever Izzy

GABE & IZZY
ANTI-BULLYING PLEDGE

www.gabeandizzy.com

I understand bullying is picking on someone and being mean to him or her over and over again. I know that bullying can happen anywhere: at home, in school, on the bus, or even on cell phones and computers.

I will do my best to remember Gabe & Izzy's message and put myself in someone else's shoes before I speak or act, so I won't hurt others with my words and actions.

I believe that EVERYONE should enjoy school and feel safe every day.

I now understand empathy and compassion, and that bullying is hurtful and a cruel CHOICE.

I will not be a bystander, but will always STAND UP AND SPEAK UP AGAINST BULLYING, as long as I feel the situation is safe. Otherwise, I will tell or get an adult.

Signature _____

Chapter One

DANCING

I was a dancer.

At dance class, I steadied myself at the barre as I watched myself in the wall-size mirror. I'd correct the angle of my pointed toe and pull my shoulders into perfect posture. I wore a pink ribbon neck-lace with a pair of tiny pink ballet shoes around my neck, to show everyone that dancing was the thing closest to my heart.

I was a dancer.

By the time I was twelve, I'd danced tap, ballet, and jazz. All the performances meant extra rehearsals and late nights. I didn't mind—it only meant I got to dance more. Hours of practice left my legs aching and my feet sore. But I had never been happier. I was a dancer.

I sparkled in a gold costume with a frilly skirt and a black sequined belt. I graduated from flat tap shoes to high-heeled ones and thought no one had ever looked better. I prepared for my test to graduate from ballet slippers to toe shoes, dreaming of their elegant ribbons, which I would wrap around my ankles. One day I'd be onstage in front of a cheering audience. I was sure of it. I'd wear beautiful costumes just like the ones I'd seen when I went to watch *The Nutcracker* with Corine, my Big Sister from the Big Brothers/Big Sisters program. I was almost eleven then—a little dancer from Fenton, Michigan, with big dreams.

In the meantime, I practiced at home. Outside my bedroom there was a closet with double, sliding, mirrored doors. Those mirrors became my personal dance studio. For seven years, I practiced and practiced in from of those closet doors.

In my favorite move, the arabesque, I'd stretch one leg out behind me, keeping my upper body straight, one arm extended. Or I'd pirouette, spinning 360 degrees on my toes. I'd feel the air rush past my ears and wisps of hair break free from my tightly wound bun.

Those days, I thought I was honing my grace and my timing, but I was really perfecting my balance. Balance is the key to holding poses and mastering all the movements that create steps and positions. I didn't realize then how easily balance had come to me—or how hard I'd have to fight to keep it.

Chapter Two

LOSING BALANCE

When I was twelve and my little sister Caitlin was around four, I went with my family to see my uncle and aunt get married. It was one of those perfect May weddings on a sunny afternoon. We were surrounded by red and white roses and loved ones, ready to celebrate.

But the sunny mood clouded when my grandfather, Papa, came to my mother at the reception. "Rhonda Kay," he said, "I'm concerned about Gabe. I can't be sure, but I think she may have gotten into the spiked punch bowl!" He'd noticed me trip, and he'd seen that I swayed when I walked.

When I came into a room, he saw that I gripped the doorframe tightly to help me keep my balance.

Mom laughed. "I don't think so, Dad."

But he wouldn't let it drop. "Well, something isn't right, Rhonda. She's not acting normal. Her balance is off."

"She wouldn't do anything like that," Mom insisted. "Dad, there's just no way."

Mom looked over at me, but she didn't notice anything wrong. Surely I couldn't have served myself the wrong punch by accident; the bowls were clearly marked. And she knew I wouldn't drink alcohol on purpose. I'd just finished the DARE (Drug Abuse Resistance Education) program at school and knew what drinking could do to you.

My mom put it out of her mind. I was fine. She was sure of it.

But Papa wasn't the only one who'd noticed that something odd was happening when it came to my balance. I'd noticed, too. When I was in choir class in seventh grade and practicing for a concert, I was assigned a place to stand on the very top row of the bleachers. Sometimes I felt unsteady making my way up to my spot. Not a big deal, but I mentioned it to my mom. She thought

I was probably just going through an awkward stage. Kids did, as they grew. So I didn't let it concern me.

Tripping once or twice? Feeling off balance as I climbed up a set of bleachers? These were little things, easy to ignore. Nothing you'd go to the doctor for.

That's what we all thought.

Then, a few months later, Mom got a phone call from my father, Dennis. It had been years since I'd seen him. He had visitation rights, but he rarely used them. Once, when I was three, he'd promised to pick me up for the weekend. I stayed by the front window all day with my little suitcase packed, waiting for the father who never came.

Now he didn't say "Hi" or "How are you?" Simply, "Rhonda, I would like to see Gabe."

Mom was stunned. "It's been years, Dennis. Why do you want to see Gabe now?"

"Well, it's about time, don't you think?"

Mom was cautious. "Can I ask you a question, Dennis?"

"Okay."

"Do you have a dog?"

Confused, he said, "Yes, I have two. Why do you ask?"

"Do you love them?"

"Yes."

"Do you let them out of their cages and feed them every day?"

"Yes. What are you getting at, Rhonda?"

"My daughter should be treated better than a dog. You're welcome to come back into her life, but please don't walk out on her again and leave her in a cage, wondering why her father has abandoned her for another twelve years."

An uncomfortable silence hung on the line before Mom said, "I'll talk to Gabe and see if she wants to see you. If she does, we'll set up a meeting."

I agreed to go on a visit. But my father was a stranger to me. I wasn't even sure what to call him. His wife, Tammy, pressured me to say "Dad." How could I? Mostly, I referred to him as "Dennis."

Still, weren't we family? Shouldn't we all just get along in some strange, mysterious way?

We didn't. I was alone in a stranger's house. Nobody spent much time with me. I couldn't relax. I was even afraid to open the refrigerator and get something to eat or drink.

Dennis and Tammy took me to the mall. They wanted to buy me things they thought I should want: different clothes and makeup. They took me to a salon and had my long blond hair cut short, to the chin. I didn't even recognize myself in the mirror.

Tammy made sure I knew I wasn't to expect this kind of treatment every time I visited. That was more than fine with me. To be honest, I didn't even want to come back. This visit wasn't what I'd been hoping for. It would be okay with me if we never repeated it.

Afterward, Dennis took me home. He sat with my mother and me at the kitchen table, and my mom was at a loss for words. I'd been away from home two days, and she hardly recognized me.

Dennis didn't have a problem finding something to say. He hadn't wanted to get to know me after all. He'd only wanted to check out some rumors he'd heard from other relatives. Rumors about my health.

When I went to my room, Dennis told my mom that Tammy had noticed I had trouble squeezing toothpaste out of the tube. His brother, my uncle, thought I might have some kind of neurological issue, problems with the way my nerves were bringing signals to and from my brain. Dennis's brother was taking his son, who was suffering from headaches, to a doctor about twenty minutes away, and Dennis wanted that doctor to see me as well.

My mom was stunned. Dennis thought he got a voice in my health care after just one weekend visit? But I was on his insurance plan. Mom let him have his way.

Dennis came with me and my mom to my first doctor's appointment, and told the doctors he'd noticed that my balance and coordination didn't seem normal. The doctor checked my reflexes and ordered a series of tests. Then his office called, and asked Dennis, my mom, and me to come back in for a talk.

Everything was normal, the doctor said. Maybe I just needed some kind of exercise program to improve my coordination.

Mom politely agreed, but she was confused. An exercise program? For the last seven years I'd eaten and breathed ballet, jazz, and tap. How much more exercise could I need?

Then, a week later, a second call came. "I'm really sorry," said the voice on the other line, "but there has been a terrible mistake. Our office staff mixed up Gabrielle's test results with another patient who has the same last name." That other patient, I found out later, was my cousin, who was being tested for headaches. "I'm really sorry to have to tell you this," the voice went on, "but Gabrielle's test results came out abnormal."

Suddenly, this wasn't about small problems, such as tripping when I walked or squeezing toothpaste from a tube. This could be something big. My mom was scared for me, but she kept her worry to herself. She didn't want to tell me I might have a serious health problem until the doctors could do more tests, until we knew for sure.

So she simply let me know that I had another appointment, three months later, with a specialist. I knew that I was going for some more tests and that Dennis would be there, but I didn't know why. In my mind I was a perfectly normal twelve-year-old girl.

A gentle nurse came to get me and took me down the hall for one of my tests. As my mother watched me walk away, she noticed for the first time the changes that everyone else had seen. The way I walked was different. My feet were wide apart, with my right foot turned out. It was hard for me to keep myself balanced, and without knowing it, I'd changed my gait to help.

There really was something wrong with me.

My mom could not look away until I disappeared around a corner. When she could not see me any longer, she went and called her mother, and told her the news. But my grandmother—who I called my mima—could barely believe anything was wrong with me; she hadn't seen the things that others had been seeing.

That day the doctor suspected that I had Friedreich's ataxia, a serious disease of the central nervous system. The nerves in the spinal cord slowly decay. It becomes hard to speak or walk. The disease can even affect the heart.

FA is progressive; that means the symptoms slowly but surely become worse over time. A person with FA usually ends up in a wheelchair ten or fifteen years after things first start to go wrong. Sometimes sooner. There's no cure. You can't take a pill for FA and get better. There isn't any better.

The doctor's suspicions were right. I had Friedreich's ataxia. But I didn't know, not at first. The doctor didn't tell me, and my mom couldn't bear to.

For six months after my diagnosis, I had no idea anything was really wrong with me. I didn't yet

FRIEDREICH'S ATAXIA

Ataxia is a general term for a physical condition where the brain cannot coordinate all the different muscle groups that work together to allow smooth, coordinated movement. A person with ataxia walks and moves with difficulty and may look "wobbly" or "jerky."

Friedreich's ataxia is caused by an abnormal copy of a single gene inside the body's cells. It affects roughly one in every 50,000 people. Some of the symptoms are:
• Slurred speech
• Changes in vision, particularly color vision
• Hearing loss
• Involuntary eye movements
• Loss of coordination and balance. A person with FA falls often. Difficulty with movement and walking gets worse over time.

- Muscle weakness
- Some people with FA develop diabetes or heart disease

FA affects the section of the brain that controls movement and balance. It does not affect the brain in other ways, or make a difference in a person's ability to think.

Right now, there is no cure for FA. Speech therapy and physical therapy may help make the symptoms less serious. Walkers and wheelchairs may help someone with FA move more easily.

Sources:
http://www.ncbi.nlm.nih.gov/pubmedhealth/PMH0002384/
http://www.curefa.org/whatis.html
http://mda.org/disease/friedreichs-ataxia/overview

know how much this disease was going to take away from me—my ability to walk, run, ride a bike, and, most of all, dance. And I didn't know how hard I'd try to keep all of those things in my life. FA wasn't going to take anything away from me without a fight.

Christmas came and went. As far as I knew, nothing had changed. My mom was still hesitating, still not sure what to do. How could she find the words to tell me I would never be a dancer? Instead, I'd be a person in a wheelchair. And I'd stay there for the rest of my life.

Her stomach ached, just thinking of breaking that news to me.

Maybe, my mom thought, she shouldn't tell me at all, or not for years. Maybe she should simply let me live my life for as long as possible, until my symptoms got so bad no one could ignore them anymore. Or maybe she would wake up one day and find out that she'd dreamed the whole thing. That nothing was wrong with me at all. That I was perfectly fine.

But my mom slowly realized that she was not dreaming. This was real. And she had to face her fear. No matter how hard it would be for her, she needed to tell me the truth.

Three days after my thirteenth birthday, both of my parents, along with my aunt, sat down with me at the kitchen table. They told me what the doctors had told them.

I cried. "Am I going to have to quit dancing?" It was the first question I asked.

Mom hated to tell me, but she got the words out. "Yes, Gabe. This is already affecting the way you walk."

I had to know. "Am I going to have to spend the rest of my life in a wheelchair?"

Mom was in tears. "One day, Gabe."

The news was more than I could bear. My tears dried up. I made my way to my bedroom and shut the door. I threw a china doll my mother had bought me against the wall and watched as it broke into pieces. I felt as though my life was shattered, just like that doll.

The next day I refused to go to school. Mom wasn't sure what to do. She asked a school counselor to come to the house. I didn't want to talk to her about having Friedreich's ataxia. I didn't even want to think about it.

In one day I'd gone from being (in my own mind, at least) perfectly healthy to being someone with a terrifying disease that was only going to get worse and worse. It was almost impossible to believe. Maybe I didn't *have* to believe it. If I shut myself away behind my bedroom door and refused to say a word about it, I could push the news away. I could almost convince myself that this wasn't actually happening. I just wanted this counselor to go away.

But my mom let the woman come to our home and into my bedroom. She was there to help, but I didn't think she could. How could she understand what I felt? She was older, an adult. She was a stranger. I didn't know her, and she didn't know me. But she told me a lot about things that happened in her own childhood—like the fact that she had had polio as a child and now walked with a limp—and I began to soften. Maybe, just maybe, I could talk to her a little about what it was like to suddenly be told I had a disease that would change my whole life.

It helped me to feel safe opening up when she promised me that whatever we talked about would be confidential, just between her and me.

She lied.

As if being told that I would end up in a wheelchair wasn't bad enough, when I returned to school the following day, it was obvious that the counselor had been talking. One of the girls in my class came up to me that morning and wanted to know something. "Do you have AIDS, Gabe?"

I knew how she'd found out. But I asked anyway. "Why would you say that?"

"The counselor told me you have a disease," she admitted.

I don't think the counselor meant to hurt me. But finding out she had betrayed my trust and told people about my situation was extremely painful. From then on, I never confided in a teacher or a counselor again. In truth, I didn't want to talk to *anyone* about my disease. To talk about it would make it seem real, and I didn't want it to be real.

Who would?

Posted by Hayley

Today, you and Izzy visited my school. . . . I thought that the presentation would be just another "No bullying" or "Stay drug-free" assembly, but this was different. I liked hearing from someone who actually knew what she was talking about. I talked to you after the presentation and asked you what it was like when you found out that you were no longer able to dance. I know, and told you, that if I found out I couldn't dance anymore, I would be completely heartbroken. I would like you and your mom to know that from now on, I will be dancing for you. God bless you and Izzy.

Chapter Three

BULLIED

I saw Dennis only a few more times. After a while it became clear that he didn't have much interest in staying in touch. It would be up to my mom and me to deal with my illness together.

A few weeks after learning about my diagnosis, I sat near a table while Mom stood behind me and brushed my blond hair. I'd been growing it out since Dennis had it cut. It wasn't as long as it used to be, but it was long enough to make me enjoy how it felt as my mom pulled the brush through the strands.

"Gabe," Mom said, "I've been thinking about your illness and how it has been impacting you."

I could tell this was going to be another "Mom talk." But since I really liked the way she brushed my hair, I stayed and listened.

"We know that eventually you won't be able to walk, Gabe," she went on, "but I want us to take this one day at a time. We aren't going to keep looking back. We've got to go forward and make every day count. Each new day we have together is the best one we will have."

"That's fine with me, Mom," I answered. "But I need everyone to do something for me. I don't want anyone to mention anything associated with my disease. I can't dwell on it. If I do, I'll get depressed."

Mom knew exactly what I meant. The words *wheelchair, walker, cane, leg brace,* or *Friedreich's ataxia* were not to be mentioned in the house. I wouldn't even let family members watch the Jerry Lewis telethon while I was around. It scared me too much. I couldn't handle watching others suffer, knowing that one day I would be just like them.

So I didn't talk about it. Ever. Somehow, deep inside, I believed that if I never said a single word about my ataxia or anything associated with it, nothing bad would happen to me. My symptoms would not get worse. I'd still be able to do every-thing I'd always done. It didn't make sense, but I needed to think that way to keep myself going. Otherwise, I might just give up.

Mom wanted me to know I wasn't the only one out there with FA. She got the names of several other teens who had the same disease. But after a few arranged meetings, I told Mom I didn't want to hang out with them anymore. It wasn't that I thought I was better than the other kids. But it seemed to me that all they wanted to talk about was the disease we shared. I didn't. I didn't want to think about it at all.

I had other things on my mind anyway. September was coming. I would begin eighth grade, and I'd do it in a new school, one that went from eighth to twelfth grade. I'd be in high school.

It would be my first year in a new school, with new faces. It would also be my first new school year with Friedreich's ataxia. I was positive no one would want to be my friend if they knew about my disease. Why would they like someone so different?

I set a goal for myself: I'd make it through high school without using a wheelchair. No canes, either. No braces, no walkers. My school was a small one, and I knew I would stand out if I was using any kind of adaptive equipment to help myself get around. Standing out was definitely not what I wanted. A few close friends did know about my disease, but as for the rest of the kids—I was going to make sure they saw me looking as "normal" as possible.

It shouldn't be that hard, right? All I had to do was walk down a hallway. Sit at a desk. Answer the teacher's questions.

All of that would have been easy for me once. But it wasn't anymore. Walking was beginning to get difficult. Stairs became a struggle. Bleachers were worse. My balance was off, and it got easier and easier for me to trip and fall. My voice changed, too. Words came out sounding odd or awkward, as if I were just learning to talk.

But none of this was obvious to me. I ignored every symptom of FA, and I hoped the other kids would do the same.

They didn't. They saw clearly all of the things I refused to see. I thought I was just Gabe, the person I'd always been. My classmates saw a girl who struggled to walk. Who slurred her words.

Whose grades were slipping because she had to concentrate so hard on every move.

When they looked at me, the others kids saw somebody who was different.

I couldn't hide the way I walked and talked. Even my grades were not a secret. The teachers gave corrected assignments and homework to the first kids in the rows, and the papers would be handed back. Everybody got a chance to glance at the grades of the people sitting behind them. I hated that, hated knowing that the kids in front of me could see how I'd done. They thought I wasn't smart. I was. I just didn't have as much energy to spend on schoolwork as I used to, because I had to work so hard on seeming "normal" every minute.

My grades, my speech, my unsteady gait—all of it made me a target.

When I heard the first few snide comments, I assumed I was just getting teased because I was new. But over months and months, things got worse, and I began to wonder if they were on to me. Did they know my deep, dark secret?

Everybody has a few bad moments in high school, moments they hate to remember. An insult. A cruel remark. A spiteful laugh. But for me, these

WHAT IS BULLYING?

"Bullying is unwanted, aggressive behavior, often among schoolchildren, that involves a real or perceived power imbalance. The behavior is repeated, or has the potential to be repeated, over time."

This definition is from StopBullying.gov, a Web site managed by the U.S. Department of Health and Human Services. Simply put, it means that bullying is mean behavior that happens over and over to a person who can't defend him- or herself, or who doesn't believe that he or she can. In some instances, the individual who is doing the bullying is not aware of how his or her actions are perceived.

Source:
www.stopbullying.gov/what-is-bullying/definition/index.html

WHAT DOES BULLYING LOOK LIKE?

A bully can use words by:
- Teasing or taunting
- Calling names
- Making unwanted sexual comments
- Making threats
- Using racial slurs or stereotypes
- Mocking someone's sexual orientation

A bully can use friendships and relationships by:
- Leaving someone out
- Telling other children not to be friends with the victim
- Spreading rumors
- Embarrassing someone in public

A bully can use force by:
- Hitting, kicking, or punching
- Spitting
- Tripping or pushing
- Stealing or breaking the victim's possessions

moments happened every single day, often many times a day. From eighth grade to twelfth, I don't remember a day I wasn't teased.

I'd had some experience with bullies before. Back in seventh grade, there had been a girl in my choir class; I'll call her Rose. I'd walk into class, ready to sing. And Rose would start in on whatever I was wearing. My jeans weren't designer jeans; why couldn't I wear what was cool? When I finally found a pair of designer jeans on the clearance rack, I was excited to get to school and show them off. But when I did, there was more laughter. Rose told me they were boys' jeans! I shoved the pants into a drawer and never wore them again. Mom kept asking me why I didn't wear the jeans I'd begged her to buy, but how could I tell her I'd been teased for wearing boys' clothes?

Posted by Anna

Gabe, I really think that you are right, that no one deserves to be bullied. I don't know why anyone would bully you, I mean, you're pretty, and it surprises me that people were mean to you. I know how you feel about being bullied. People bully me because they think that

I'm ugly. I'm really tall so my pants are always too short on me. People are also mean to me because of that. I know I'm pretty, but people still call me ugly.

When it came to the seating chart, my luck was bad; Rose sat right behind me. This gave her the chance to whack me on the head with her thick music book. I didn't want to admit to anyone what was going on, but I couldn't handle getting hurt over and over. I would cringe, waiting for the blow to fall, and then for the laughter to start. Everyone watching seemed to find it amusing. Why was it funny, watching someone get hurt?

Finally, I told my mom what was happening.

My mom knew Rose's mother, and she called her up; the woman said she'd talk to her daughter. And Rose apologized to me. No more blows on the head with a heavy hardcover textbook.

But in high school, things were more complicated. I wasn't facing just one mean girl. I was locked in a battle with my own body, struggling to do the everyday things that all the other kids did without thinking—that *I* used to do without thinking. And at the same time, it began to feel as if the whole school had turned against me.

WHO GETS BULLIED?

Almost anyone can be bullied. But children with disabilities or special health needs are more likely to be attacked. So are children who stutter, stammer, or have difficulties with speech.

I wasn't the only target of the bullies in my school. I remember another boy who had cerebral palsy and needed crutches to walk. He would be sitting and reading out loud to his aide, and some of the other students would steal his crutches. He couldn't walk without them, or not easily. It was such a cruel thing to do.

Source:
http://www.stopbullying.gov/at-risk/groups/special-needs/BullyingTipSheet.pdf

Again and again, a kid would cup his or her hand around his or her jaw, moving it back and forth to mock my shaky speech. There are times that my ataxia makes me stare off into space, and other students would mimic my vacant look.

As my balance got worse and my muscles got weaker, the hallways began to seem endless. Even opening my locker was a struggle, and it was common for someone to come along and slam the door shut just as I'd finally gotten it open. One boy even reached in over my head to snatch the CDs I kept on the top shelf. He waved them in front of me, teasing and taunting, and then just walked away. I never did get them back.

One day the teachers told us to go outside for a class photo. Such a simple thing—walk out the door, sit on the bleachers, smile. But it was not simple at all for me. To get where we were going, we had to follow a gravel driveway. I stared at that driveway with dread. They might as well have asked me to make my way through a swamp with mud a mile deep. It was hard enough to walk on a flat surface; that shifting, treacherous gravel was sure to trip me. But I had no choice. All the other kids were already on their way. To say I couldn't do it would make me stand out—something I was trying so hard to avoid.

I began walking. With every step, I pictured myself falling in front of my whole class. How humiliating. What a freak I'd look like, flat on my face in the gravel. The thought of it made me want to die.

But I made it at last, still on my feet. I got to the bleachers, safe. But the fear of embarrassing myself in front of everyone had been nearly as bad as the falling itself. And that fear never really went away.

I was scared of falling for a good reason. I knew that, if I fell, I'd be laughed at. I knew because it happened. Often. Once I was struggling up a short flight of three steps when I tripped and fell, right in view of a boy who loved to tease me. I knew the story would go all around school, that he'd never let me or anybody else forget it. Gabe Ford couldn't even make it up the stairs.

I didn't always fall down by myself. Kids loved to step on the backs of my heels to throw me off balance. Someone would push me from behind to watch me stumble, or shove me into another kid, laughing. My books would be knocked from my hands, and someone might kick them for fun and watch as I scrambled after them.

Missiles flew at me—spit wads, eraser tips, paper clips, pencils, chalk, bits of chewed-up plastic. They'd hit my face or stick in my hair. And the ugly words flew, too.

"Are you drunk?"

"You're walking like you're drunk."

"You talk like you're drunk! You really ought to lay off the booze, Gabe!"

Of course I wasn't drunk. Ataxia made me trip and fall, made me slur and stumble over my words. But I wasn't about to tell that to these kids who took joy in mocking me.

Maybe they would have let up on me if I'd explained why I walked and talked the way I did. Or maybe it would only have given them something new to tease me about. I couldn't be sure, so I kept my mouth shut. In any case, I didn't like talking about ataxia, and I didn't think I should have to. My health was my own business. Should I really make an announcement to the whole school about something I wanted to keep private, just so I could walk down the hall in peace?

Even after the bell rang for school to end,

the bullying wasn't over. My shortest route home was along a busy road with no sidewalks. I walked slowly along the bumpy, gravelly shoulder, concentrating hard to keep from falling. A pack of kids would be at my heels or on the other side of the street, and the insults kept coming. "What's the matter, Gabe?" somebody would ask. "Got a brain tumor?" Or they teased me about my acne. "Pizza face!" Well, of course I had acne—everybody did. We were teenagers. But somehow my acne made me a target for bullying in ways other people weren't.

The bullying even spread to touch my little sister. I'll never forget the day Caitlin, just seven years old, ran off of the school bus in tears. "Are we trailer trash?" she asked, sobbing. That was a common insult at school, and it wasn't directed only at our family. Right across from the modular home park where we lived was a beautiful lake lined with big houses, even mansions. Our school felt divided between the two neighborhoods, and the kids who lived on the lake looked down on those of us who lived in the park, even though they had no good reason. I loved that park; it was my home, and I wasn't ashamed to live there.

I miss it to this day. I was only sorry to see my little sister crying so hard, suddenly afraid that her own home was an awful place. Just because of a single cruel name.

Posted by Bailee

Hi, Gabe! Thank you very much for coming to my school. You touched many people's hearts and taught a lot of students that you should not bully. I think it is amazing how you can talk to anyone about being bullied or about your disease. One time when I was in fifth grade a kid was calling me a slave on Martin Luther King Jr. Day. I took it seriously, but I think you inspired me to not care what others think about me but what I think about myself and be happy for who you are and not let people hate you for who you are.

It hurt, seeing Caitlin so upset. Harsh words stung, whether they were thrown at me or my sister. But threats were more frightening. "My friend likes the boy you've been talking to," a girl told me during lunch one day. I was sitting in the gym, minding my own business, when she came up to me. "If you don't stop talking to him,

I'm going to slap you," she warned me. Slap me? For what? Talking to a boy I thought of only as a friend? Then she told me I was ugly.

In biology class, two girls hovered over me, repeating a rumor that I'd accused the two of them of copying off another girl's homework and telling the teacher. I swore it wasn't true. But they didn't listen and threatened to beat me up. It looked to me like they meant it.

I needed help. I was sick and tired of being bullied. But I had no idea where to go or whom to ask. I knew my mom would be furious if she learned I was being teased, insulted, pushed, and threatened every day, several times a day. She would go to my school and speak to my principal, I was certain. If kids found out she'd done that, would they make fun of me even more?

I could have told a teacher or a counselor, instead of my mom. But which one? If there had been a particular adult at my school whose job it was to deal with bullying, I might have found a way to talk to him or her. But there wasn't such a person. Nobody was talking openly about bullying at my school.

Besides, I really wasn't sure which adult I could trust. Back in seventh grade, I'd confided in the school counselor about my illness. She was the first adult, outside of my own family, that I'd told. And she'd betrayed my confidence, talking to other students about me. Would the teachers at my high school do the same? Maybe so. I didn't want to risk it, letting my secret out.

It came down to this: I didn't really believe adults would help me. I was sure that some teachers noticed that I was being bullied, but they didn't want to get involved. I felt as though I had no safe place to go, where I could talk to others about my troubles. Silently, I tried to handle it all myself.

I was just one girl surrounded by a group of bullies. How could I make anything change?

Posted by Kayla

I'm very glad you came to our school. Your assembly really made me think about bullying. . . . It also taught me to report bullying the next time I see it, and I see it often. I'm going to report bullying the next time I see it because I don't want someone to feel alone like Gabe did.

Chapter Four

MAKING IT THROUGH

When I was growing up, I used to look forward to my high school years, and all the fun I'd have. But instead of driving, dating, playing sports, and joining clubs, I'd ended up with abuse, harassment, and fear. High school was no longer a dream. It had turned into a living nightmare.

Since I didn't know how to ask for help—and since I didn't want to be the kind of kid who *needed* help—I tried to deal with the bullying on my own. I thought if I ignored the kids who picked on me, eventually they would stop. Wrong. I thought if I was nice to others, they'd start being nice to me. Wrong.

There were times I wanted to fight back. I thought about hitting someone, or throwing an insult back at those who bullied me. But I didn't. My mom had told me that if anyone ever made fun of me, to look them in the eye and tell them what they were doing was wrong and hurtful, and then to walk away. She said I should try to be the bigger person. "Maybe those kids don't understand what they are doing," she told me, "how much it hurts, and the damage it can do. But maybe, someday, they will.

"Everyone in life goes through hard times and trials, and someday hard times will come to those kids, too," my mom went on. "Maybe when they're still teenagers, maybe when they're adults. Perhaps their hard times will be like yours; perhaps they will be different. They may have children one day, Gabe, with a disability. Or they may have children bullied. Then they will remember you. Hopefully, they will feel remorse, and teach their children not to bully other classmates."

I recalled a time when I was in second grade, long before my health problems began. The school I was attending was all white, except for a single black boy in my class. One day, we were standing in the lunch line, and one of my friends turned to him and said, "You are not welcome in our school and we are not going to play with you." Though she was my friend, I knew that what she had said was wrong and hurtful. I turned to the boy and told him, "Yes, you *are* welcome in this school, and *I* will play with you." Another time, my classmates were excluding a boy who was overweight from playing games with them at recess. Since they would not play with him, I did.

Even at that young age, it seemed so easy to do the right thing. So why wouldn't anyone do it for me now that I was being bullied?

I thought about my mom's words, and I tried hard not to let the kids who bullied me turn me into a bully, too. But nothing I tried seemed to make things better. So I just went back to school day after day, full of dread. Deep down inside I felt angry, and there were even times I didn't want to live, if life meant going through this. But I wasn't going to drop out. That wasn't an option in our family; we were expected to finish high school. I told myself each day was one day closer to graduation, gritted my teeth, and endured.

In high school, my rules for dealing with bullies could be boiled down to one phrase: be invisible.

I didn't raise my hand in class. I tried to avoid reading aloud in my shaky, wobbly voice. I started to stay away from groups of kids whenever I could. Bathrooms were dangerous—too many girls, no teachers nearby. Pep rallies were nerve-wracking. What if a popular kid, knowing Gabe was easy to pick on, decided to make a spectacle of me in front of the entire school? The cafeteria made me anxious. I often took my lunch to a classroom and ate with a teacher nearby, feeling, for the moment, safe.

But I wasn't safe, not really.

My school had big windows with wide window seats; all the kids would sit there when they had a few free minutes. But if I ever settled down to get a little rest, a boy (let's call him Jason) might see me. Jason got some kind of thrill out of slamming his fist on the outside of my thigh. I tried to avoid him, but his locker was close to mine, and he was in many of my classes; I couldn't stay out of his way forever. And whenever I did see him, I was vulnerable—especially when I was sitting in those window seats waiting for my mom to pick me up after school.

One day, Mom noticed the bruises on my leg. I didn't want to tell her what had happened, so I quietly slipped into my bedroom. She was right on my heels, and she wanted the truth. At last I told her.

Back in seventh grade, when Rose had been hitting me with her music book, I'd learned the most important thing about fighting bullies that anyone can learn: speak up. Be loud. Don't just take the abuse.

Now Mom gave me a second chance to learn that lesson. She went straight to the phone and called the assistant principal. But it didn't seem like he wanted to get involved. He asked Mom what she'd like him to do.

"You're the assistant principal," Mom answered. "I was thinking you would tell me!" But he had no ideas to offer. "I would like this young man called to the office and spoken to," Mom insisted. "And I also think he should apologize to Gabe and promise he'll stop his behavior."

The assistant principal agreed. He said he'd call back. And that call never came. Mom went over his head, right to the principal, and the principal called both Jason and me to the office. He talked to us separately, and Jason did apologize. Actually, he did more than apologize. To my shock, he began to treat me better! I saw again that speaking up is the way to handle bullies—and that, if the first person you reach out to doesn't help, it's all right to try again.

Things with Jason may have turned out better than I ever hoped, but still, school was torture for me. So I looked for happiness in other places. I did have a few good friends who didn't seem to care about my disease. I'd met Amanda in eighth grade, and we spent a lot of time together during our first few years of high school—doing homework, sending instant messages, walking down to the store for candy or soda, hanging out on her family's boat. She never seemed embarrassed by how I talked or walked, and I learned that there were other people like her. That knowledge really helped me get through my high school years.

Mom had a rule that her kids had to hold down a job as soon as they were old enough. She didn't treat me any differently. My school offered a summer job program for special needs kids, and Mom pushed me to sign up. They offered me work as a secretary for a couple of hours each morning in the bus garage, and as a janitor in the afternoon. At first I wasn't sure. Did they just feel sorry for me? Did they think I couldn't get a job anywhere else?

But I found I could do the things I was asked

EXCUSES, EXCUSES

People don't always take bullying seriously. Here are some excuses people make for bullying—and why they aren't true.

"KIDS WILL BE KIDS."

Of course kids sometimes make bad choices. Part of being a kid is making mistakes and learning from them. But that doesn't mean adults shouldn't step in and stop behavior that is hurting someone else. Kids who are bullying need adult help to learn different behavior. Kids who are bullied need adult help to defend themselves.

"HE ASKED FOR IT."

A kid may look different, act differently, dress differently. Some kids can be annoying, or even provoking. None of these things excuses bullying. No one deserves to be bullied.

"THE KIDS CAN SORT IT OUT THEMSELVES."

Ordinary bad behavior—an insult, a harsh comment, an angry reaction—may be something that kids can sort out. Bullying is different. Bullying is repeated bad behavior by someone who has power, or who seems to have power, over another. The victim of bullying doesn't believe that he or she can make the abuse stop. Adult intervention is needed.

"MAYBE HE LIKES HER!"

A teacher actually said this to my mom about Jason, the boy who punched me day after day. "Maybe the boy liked Gabe!" this teacher said, laughing. My mom had to explain things to her. Abuse is not a compliment. Getting hit is not romantic. Bullying is a way to put someone down, not to show interest. Believe me, I did not feel flattered by getting hit over and over. I just wanted it to stop.

to do: answering phones, making copies, filing, mopping floors, changing lightbulbs. Nobody called me names at work; nobody threw things at me or shoved me down. I was contributing. And people treated me as an equal, not as a victim.

In eleventh and twelfth grades, I found a new job at a grocery store, Farmer Jack's. It was another place where what I did mattered. I felt needed and wanted when I bagged people's groceries and they thanked me. Such a simple thing, but it felt so good, so right, so normal, that it kept me going when things at school were hard to bear.

My mom had made it clear to me that I was allowed to bag groceries at Farmer Jack's, but she didn't want me out on the parking lot in winter weather collecting the shopping carts. She was worried that I couldn't keep my balance and I'd take a bad fall on the asphalt.

So she wasn't pleased at all when she arrived one icy, snowy day to pick me up, and found me doing my best to gather carts with the snow blowing in my face. My eyelashes were thick with snowflakes, as if I had on white mascara. But I was doing my job, and I was happy.

Mom, however, wasn't. "Gabe!" she bellowed. "What are you doing?"

I looked at her, my hood covering my forehead, my red face full of snow, and said, "Let me do this while I can, Mom!"

She understood that I was trying to do more than my job, and she didn't order me back inside. Instead, she jumped out of the car and said, "Let me help you!"

Together we gathered all of the carts, laughing as they (and we!) slipped and slid in the heavy snow. For once, I wasn't the only one fighting to keep my balance. My mom, who was trying to keep her balance and not fall, looked a lot like me. If anyone had been watching us, they would have thought I was unsteady because of the ice and snow underfoot, not because I had ataxia. What a relief, to blend in for once.

At last we shoved the wet, dripping carts toward the automatic doors, but when they hit the doormats, they rolled right back outside! Mom and I laughed until we were sure we couldn't laugh anymore.

Unfortunately, I couldn't spend all of my time at my jobs. For hours every day I had to be in school. And school wasn't just the place where I got teased, mocked, shoved, tripped, and punched day after day. It was also a place where I was reminded of other things, like dance.

I'd had to drop out of dance; I didn't have a choice. And I missed lessons something fierce. At school, I knew it was the time of year when my old friends would talk about the recitals that were coming up, and I'd feel as if I were sinking in a hole that I could never climb out of, no matter how hard I tried. My sister, Caitlin, would bring her costumes home, and while I was happy to see what they looked like, I couldn't help wishing that one of them was for me. My dance friends—and my sister—were moving forward, and I was slipping down.

At home I would look over at the bag filled with my dance clothes and shoes, still hanging on the doorknob. Then I would look at the old worn ballet shoes that my mom had put up on my wall. Day after day, those sights reminded me that my world was spinning in a direction I hated. Dance had been a huge part of who I was, and overnight it had been snatched away from me.

Another reminder—as if I needed one—was coming up as my senior year neared its end. Prom was approaching. When I was younger and used to go shopping with my mom, I'd notice the pretty prom dresses hanging in store windows and dream of the day I would grow up and pick one out for myself. Nothing else about high school had turned out like I'd imagined. What about prom? Was that going to be a big disappointment, too?

One day a group of kids—most of them on the hockey team—approached me in art class. One boy's family was hosting a foreign exchange student, "Nicolas." Nicolas had no date for the prom, his host brother told me. Why didn't I ask him to go?

I'd never been to a prom. This would be my last chance. Maybe, just maybe, Nicolas actually wanted what his host brother told me he did. Maybe he needed a date, just like I did. It took me a couple of days to work up the nerve, but I did it. I walked right up to Nicolas in the lunchroom and asked him out.

He turned me down. Every kid standing around burst into laughter. They'd known all along he would say no.

Getting turned down for a date was bad enough. But getting rejected like that, in front of a crowd, all of them in on the joke? I wanted to crawl in a hole and never come out. How could I face any of those kids again? Once more, I was the girl it was easy to pick on. The idea of going on a date with Gabe? It just made everybody laugh.

It would have been easy to stay home, after that. And prom was just the kind of thing I'd ordinarily hide from: big groups of kids, not many teachers to keep an eye on things. But this time I wasn't going to let bullies keep me from doing something I wanted.

A friend of mine, Aaron, said he would go with me. Getting ready—that was the fun part. At last I had my own prom dress: celery green, down to the floor. I put on my makeup just right. My nails were done, my hair was piled up in curls on top of my head. I smiled for the pictures. I was going to prom, just like everybody else.

I was glad I'd done it, but it still wasn't easy. I could dress up, I could spend the night at a party, but the one thing I couldn't do was dance. You can't imagine how much I wanted to be a girl dancing at her prom, just like all the others. When I tried, I fell. Aaron was sweet and held me up, but it wasn't the same, and it wasn't what I longed to be doing. I could hear the beat, and I wanted to move to it, but my body wouldn't let me. All I could think about was how my body used to move to the music!

Prom was not the last moment of the year. Graduation was coming—at last. The end of high school, surely, meant the end of bullying. It was a wonderful thought until I went into the auditorium with my class to practice our graduation march and saw all the steps leading down to our seats, plus more stairs up and down from the stage.

Stairs. Why did there have to be stairs? How would I ever make it up and down? My whole class would be there; their parents and families would be watching. What if I fell one last time? What if I made a fool of myself right in front of everyone?

After I calmed down a little, I took a closer look and told myself not to panic. If I concentrated, if I tried hard, surely I could get up to the stage and down again without falling flat on my face. I'd gotten this far; I'd made it through high school. I could do this one last thing.

At least that was what I told myself.

Graduation day came. The doors opened into the auditorium. This was it! My heart began to beat fast. The empty auditorium, where we'd practiced only a few days before, was now full of people. The music, "Pomp and Circumstance," seemed so loud as we entered. My hands began to sweat. I had to make it to my seat without falling and embarrassing myself. I'd never forgive myself if I didn't. I took a few deep breaths and began walking toward my chair.

Then a step caught me by surprise. My ankle twisted and I fell sprawling. My uncle came running to help me, but that was the last thing I wanted. Now everybody was staring at me—at least, that's what it felt like.

I made it to my seat and sat there through the ceremony and the speeches without hearing a word. My ankle hurt horribly, but all I could think about was making it across the stage without falling a second time. Did I look like a complete fool earlier? Would I go down in history as the girl who ruined graduation? If only I could run out of that auditorium, but no—I couldn't turn back now. I was going to walk up those stairs, get my diploma, and walk down.

And I was going to do it on my own. No canes for me. No braces. Above all, no wheelchairs. Not today.

When my name was finally called, I stood up and moved toward the stairs. My ankle ached with every step. I ignored it. Step by step, I got up the stairs. The minute I had my diploma in my hand, relief washed over me. I'd done it, what I'd vowed in eighth grade. I'd made it through high school on my own two feet.

But the night wasn't over.

There was a lock-in at school, a giant party, meant to keep kids safe on graduation night. My ankle was killing me from my fall, but I was determined to go. I rarely went to any school events; this would be my last chance. I wanted to spend the night with the few friends I had at school, and they wanted me to attend. For once I was going to be like any other senior. I didn't let Mom know how much I was hurting.

The gym had been transformed into an Amazon rain forest. It felt magical. On this night, the first night of our grown-up lives, anything was possible—at least that's how it seemed.

And something remarkable did happen. Only one kid made fun of me for falling. I wasn't surprised; this boy made fun of me all the time. His teasing was constant; it was relentless. When I think of the people who tormented me in high school, I can still see his face. I've forgiven him, but it hasn't been easy; the memory of his abuse can still get under my skin. He has a lot to live with, and I hope he is sorry for how he treated me.

Apart from that one kid, however, everybody

seemed ready to have fun. For once, that included me. There were tricycle races, potato sack races, a poker room, dancing beneath a giant disco ball. My ankle kept me from doing too many of these things, though. I stood and talked to friends, and toward the end of the night I looked around for a place to sit.

A raffle drawing was going on. A table was covered with prizes donated by the local shops, and a friend told me she'd seen a Detroit Red Wings hockey jersey. She knew I was a huge Red Wings fan. What a wonderful prize for some-body, I thought. But I never imagined hearing the announcer call out my name as I was resting my aching foot—"Gabrielle Ford!"

I'd never won anything before in my life! I could hardly believe that I had Chris Osgood's jersey in my hand. But there was a second surprise to come.

"Way to go, Gabe!" a familiar voice cheered. "That's my girl!"

Mom came over to the table where I sat with my friends, hugged me, and took a picture of us all. Even Jason was there. We weren't the best of friends, but we could get along, and all because of what the principal had done to address his bullying.

"Mom," I asked, "why did you come to pick me up so early? I'm not ready to go home."

"I didn't plan to, Gabe, but I woke out of a deep sleep around four o'clock this morning, threw on my jeans, and drove quickly to the school. I sensed that something was wrong. Instead I had the amazing sight of watching you win Osgood's jersey. Some things are just meant to be."

After the night was over, I fell into bed and slept all day. Finally awake, in the evening, I called Mom to my room and asked, "Will you take a look at my ankle?" As soon as she did, we were off to the emergency room. My ankle was half the size of a baseball. I had a torn ligament, so the emergency room doctors put me in an air cast.

As we headed home from the hospital, I tried to imagine what life after high school would be like. I'd done it. I'd made it through twelfth grade without telling anyone the truth about having Friedreich's ataxia.

I didn't really understand it then, but hiding my ataxia from everyone in school was really a way of hiding it from myself. If I never admitted that I had FA, if I never talked about it, if I never gave in and used a wheelchair or a walker, then I could almost believe that I didn't actually have this disease. That I could still enjoy all the things I'd always imagined high school would bring me: driving, dates, dances, friends, fun.

But after all, high school had not been like that. And it had been such hard work, keeping my disease a secret, trying so hard to be "normal" that I could hardly be myself.

Maybe I could stop hiding now. Maybe I was free to be who I actually was, for the first time in years.

Chapter Five

CHANGES

My graduation money burned a hole in my pocket. I could hear the mall calling my name. Because of my injured ankle, I couldn't walk on my own, so Mom became my walker. She took me to the mall and wandered arm in arm with me, visiting all my favorite stores: Wilsons Leather, Macy's, Lady Foot Locker. My bags swelled with goodies—shirts, jeans, perfume, a leather coat.

We shopped till we dropped—literally. I'd taken breaks throughout the day, but by the time we were done, my right knee was aching fiercely. On the way back to the car, my knee gave out, and I slipped from Mom's arm and fell to the ground.

As it turned out, that was the last day Mom and I were able to walk through a mall together.

I'd already been forced to quit my job at Farmer Jack's. I just couldn't stand for hours on end the way I used to. After a while, it became painful for me to stand for any length of time at all. I'd go along on errands with Mom, but I'd stay in the car while she ran in and out of stores. I didn't want people to see me. My biggest fear was running into former classmates who bullied me. Staying in the car made me feel safe.

My knee was beginning to ache a lot, and my balance was getting worse. It was easy to trip over my own feet. To stay upright, I needed to hold on to something—a wall, a chair, a countertop. In fact, I wore all the wallpaper off the corner of a hallway in our house from gripping it for support.

My legs were covered with bruises from all my falls. My handwriting had once been pretty; now it looked like a scribble. My hands were unsteady when I tried to hold a cup of water, and I often spilled my drink. I hated the sound of my voice, and I wouldn't talk if my mom had her camcorder on, trying to record a family movie. I didn't want my picture taken, either. I didn't want to see myself this way.

Even such a simple thing as swallowing food became difficult. Often I'd feel a bite get lodged in my throat. I'd excuse myself and struggle to the bathroom, where I tried to remove whatever was stuck. But there were times I truly couldn't breathe, and my mom had to help me before I choked. It scared us all—myself included. I asked my mom to cut up my chicken into smaller pieces.

Doctor's appointments were a regular part of my days, but that didn't make me like them. My mom would go with me, and sometimes my high school friend Amanda would come along for support. We had drifted apart over the last few years of school, but we reunited. But most of the time, it was just Mom and me. On our way, I wouldn't talk; the car would be full of silence. And once we got to the office, I had no plans to cooperate. My doctors would always push me to use a walker, braces, handrails in the house. I wanted no part of it. I knew once I gave in to using any type of medical equipment there would be no turning back.

I was ready to hang on to the walls, scoot on my butt, or do whatever I could think of, rather than let myself be seen using any kind of adaptive equipment. Equipment would mean my condition was real. And it would also mean I'd be vulnerable. I remembered a classmate in high school with cerebral palsy; the other students used to steal his crutches and leave him helpless. I wanted no part of that kind of treatment.

I knew I was stubborn. But maybe being stubborn wasn't all bad. My doctor told me often that people with FA either fight or give in. Those who give in can be wheelchair bound within a year of getting their diagnosis. I didn't want that to be me. I wanted to walk forever, and being a fighter kept me out of a wheelchair for as long as possible.

I didn't like the changes from my disease—but they were inevitable. I wasn't ready for the other changes graduation brought. Most of my friends weren't planning to go away for college, and I was glad. Things would stay the same between us, or at least that's what I thought. But when I called them up and left messages, no one got back to me. It was as if they'd all disappeared.

Mom told me it was normal. After high school, everyone starts a new life. "They've found a new freedom they've never known before," she told me. "It's not that they don't like you, Gabe, it's just that they are finally free."

I thought to myself: yes, my friends are free

from school. But why does that mean they have to be free from me? My mom still had high school friends she stayed in touch with. I thought I'd keep my own friends for a few more years at least. But I was wrong. Was it my disease that made it so hard for them to keep in touch?

Thanks to FA, it took time to be my friend. I couldn't keep up with them when we went out; I just trailed behind. I couldn't do the things they were now doing—new jobs, college classes, new apartments or places of their own.

Would they have returned my calls if I didn't have ataxia?

I couldn't understand why my friends were so silent, and I couldn't stop asking my mom why they no longer called. One day I had friends and school-work to keep me busy—the next, I had nothing but too much time on my hands and nothing to do with it. Since I couldn't drive, I stayed home, away from the eyes I was certain gawked at me. More and more often, I found myself crying and angry.

It was lonely, being home all day with a phone that never rang. Mom and my stepfather, Rick, were at work. Papa, my mother's father, lived with us now, in his own apartment downstairs. He had moved in after Mima passed away. He'd check in on me, but I didn't talk much. I didn't have much to talk about. Caitlin was at school, and my youngest sister, Madeline, born when I was sixteen, was at day care all day long.

A new baby sister might have seemed like a blessing, but the truth is, I hadn't been too happy when I found out my mother was expecting. Rick loved sports, and secretly, I thought maybe he wanted a child who could grow up to be an athlete—unlike her oldest sister. Maybe the new baby would replace me. Maybe they'd love her more, and I'd become a burden. Maybe that's what I already was.

All of the mean comments from my old classmates began to swirl over and over in my head. Was I really what they'd always told me I was: a loser?

I'd get up in the morning and take a shower first thing. The soothing water helped fight off the dark feelings. But I could stay in the bathroom for only so long. I slept a lot—too much! Mom would come home and find me with my head on a table, or curled up asleep on the living room floor, like a small animal. She worried that what I was going through was part of my disease, and she

WHAT BULLYING CAN DO

Bullying can have serious effects. Children who have been bullied:

- Are more likely to experience depression and anxiety. This doesn't simply mean feeling sad or nervous. These emotions are normal, and they pass. But depression and anxiety are feelings that people cannot control. People suffering from depression and anxiety may get "stuck" feeling sad, lonely, or helpless for long periods of time. They sometimes change their sleeping and eating habits and lose interest in things they once enjoyed.

- Have more health problems.

- Have lower grades and test scores.

- Are more likely to hurt themselves, or think about hurting themselves.

- Are more likely to lose self-esteem and confidence.

- Participate less in school.

- Are more likely to skip or drop out of school.

Sources:
http://www.stopbullying.gov/at-risk/groups/special-needs/BullyingTipSheet.pdf
http://www.ncd.gov/publications/2011/March92011

didn't know how to help. "Look at me, Mom. Really look at me!" I yelled one day the moment she came home from work. "My body is changing so fast. I can't walk and get around like I used to. I'm ashamed of myself. Can you understand why I don't want people to see me this way? I'm so different."

Mom was surprised, but her answer was quick. "It doesn't matter what other people think, Gabe, you can't go on like this. You're robbing yourself of the life you've been given. You need to go and live it. Remember what we talked about? Don't look back on life, but look forward and make each day count. Just do your part to make the world a better place and you'll be happier."

Well, I tried. Mom had told me that I'd either need to go to school or get a job after graduation. After thinking it over, I decided to get training to become a travel agent. I studied geography, military time, airport codes, ways to book flights, car rentals, train trips, and cruises. Plus I got an introduction to places I'd love to see firsthand: India, Greece, Thailand, Egypt, Italy.

Mom and my stepfather, Rick, gave me rides to and from school. Once we were there, Mom would wrap her arm around my waist and walk me into class, right to my chair. When my legs got too wobbly, we'd laugh and act like we were dancing.

So many times, at the end of the day, she'd stoop down and say, "Get on my back; it's easier." Off we'd go, back to the car. My arms would wrap around her neck, and she'd tell me not to choke her. Sometimes I would say, "Giddy up, horsie." The laughter we shared was good for both our souls.

She knew me well. If it weren't for her, I would not have gone to school—or anywhere. I hadn't used a wheelchair yet, and I didn't plan on using one anytime soon. The idea of any of the kids from my old high school seeing me was torture. If they'd made fun of me while I was walking, what would they say if they saw me pushing myself around?

Some people told my mom that she was enabling me, letting me get away with hiding from reality. That was easy for them to say. They weren't the ones losing the ability to walk—their independence. If they'd been in my shoes, I'm pretty sure they would have wanted to walk forever, too. I didn't judge them, why did they judge me?

As long as I could, I'd do everything for myself. I knew what it was like to walk, run, ride a bike, golf, play soccer, and dance. I couldn't allow myself to dwell on the reality—that all of that was over.

As long as I could walk by holding on to the furniture, or my mom, I would.

But even with my mom to help, it wasn't easy, being out where people could see me. I was sure that, no matter where I went, everybody's eyes were on me. My family would go out to dinner, and I'd resist. Was I going to walk to a table, wobbling all the way, giving everyone in the parking lot and the restaurant a chance to stare? Not likely. Even once I got to a chair and could sit down like anybody else, the ordeal would not be over. I'd have to speak up and order a meal in the voice I couldn't count on. Would the waitress ask me to repeat my order? Would she roll her eyes at me? Would she think I wasn't smart?

I'd rather just sit in the car. And I often did. My middle sister, Caitlin, got exasperated with me. She didn't have my disease and couldn't understand how I felt. The way she saw it, any family outing might be ruined by Gabe sulking in the car or fuming at the table.

But it was hard, watching my balance and strength fade away. It was lonely watching my friends hurry off into their new, grown-up lives. And however much I loved my sister, it was painful watching Caitlin growing up into the teenager I'd wanted to be.

Caitlin was a dancer, just like I had been. She was a cheerleader, too, and pretty as well. She had friends. She went on dates. I didn't. She had the high school life I'd always wanted—and what did I have? Friedreich's ataxia.

With all this jealousy in my heart, sometimes I just didn't like my sister. I could be pure nastiness when I wanted to. And I have to admit, there were times when I wanted to.

Some of Caitlin's friends were downright scared of me. When they came over, I wasn't nice to them—in fact, I wouldn't talk to them. I was sure they were staring at me, laughing at me, just like the kids in school. So I'd usually make my way to my bedroom and close the door, shutting them out. Shutting everybody out.

There were times I was so frustrated that I'd throw something, or just fling my arm and clear a table of everything that was on it. Once I even tipped the kitchen table over. There was all this rage inside me that I had kept in from my school days, rage at what had happened to me. Any little thing could let it out.

Even when I tried to push past my fears, that

anger could still ambush me and make things tough for my family. When someone I knew slightly asked me to a New Year's party, I said I'd go. I didn't like the idea of meeting new people— they might stare, they might laugh, they might make fun of me. Even so, I found my courage and said yes. Mom had been trying to get me to face my fears. By accepting this invitation I was truly trying to, and trying hard.

But I couldn't drive myself, and Mom and Rick had plans. They were throwing a New Year's party, too. So I would need a ride. The host promised to swing by and pick me up.

It would be my first grown-up New Year's party. Despite my nerves, I was excited. I got ready early, took my shower, styled my hair, put my makeup on, and dressed up, ready for my ride to get here.

Mom cleaned the house, decorated, and set up food while I waited in my bedroom. Her guests began to arrive. I was still waiting, and starting to get worried. Nobody had come to give me a ride. Nobody had called to explain why.

How pathetic did I look, sitting all dressed up in my bedroom by myself? Did this have to happen when the house was full of people?

Eventually, I had to admit it. Nobody was

coming. I wasn't going to any party. I walked unsteadily into the living room, and Mom looked at me with sympathy.

"I know you're disappointed, Gabe," she said gently, "but you're welcome to join us."

I exploded. "Why would I want to do that, Mom?" My voice was ugly and sarcastic. Everybody could see my rage, a cover for the embarrassment that was making my cheeks burn. The room grew quiet. Too quiet. I headed for my room and spent the rest of the night alone.

My acquaintance had humiliated me. I had humiliated my mom. The next day, she told me how she felt, and that I needed to write letters to her friends, apologizing for my behavior. I didn't want to, but I knew she was right and I was wrong. I'd been hurt, but that didn't give me the right to take that hurt out on her and her friends. I'd been bullied most of my life. I didn't need to turn into a bully now. I wrote the letters.

For a long time, I was too miserable to see what my pain was doing to me—and to my family. All they wanted was for me to be with them. And I would hide instead, or lash out. It was easier to stay in my tight little world of despair.

One day Mom came into my bedroom and

asked me to go shopping with her. I said no. Again. One more *no* on top of all the others I'd been saying for so long.

Mom couldn't leave it at that. She threw her hands up into air and told me that it was a beautiful sunny day and she was going to go out and live it. I could sit inside my four bedroom walls and rot if I wanted to. The choice was mine. She walked out.

What my mom said that day in my room made me think. She was right. I wasn't living anything that could be called much of a life.

I didn't have a choice about having Friedreich's ataxia. I couldn't make my friends call me back. I couldn't give myself my sister's life. But I *could* get out of my bedroom if I wanted to. It was time to start living the life I'd been given. But to do that, I'd need a little help.

Chapter Six

BUILDING
A MYSTERY

Two years had passed since I'd graduated from high school, and I was eaten up with loneliness. I would sit with my head for hours on the kitchen table. No one was home during the day except Papa, my grandfather. He would ask me if I was okay, and I would tell him yes. Then he would go and do his yard work.

I needed a friend. Not my papa, although I loved him—something more. A friend who would be happy to see me, no matter what mood I was in. Who would stay by my side no matter what. In other words, I needed a dog. (And if that dog happened to be cute and cuddly with really long ears, so much the better.)

My uncle Bob and aunt Linda had a dog named Sox, one that I really liked. The more I thought about Sox, and about dogs in general, the more I began to believe that a dog could be a perfect best friend. Dogs are loyal, always there for you, warm and cuddly. A dog won't say mean or hurtful words. A dog doesn't judge you by your looks, or by what you can or cannot do. A dog would be with me while my family was working or going to school. It would need me as much as I needed it.

All I had to do was convince Mom.

I knew she loved me with all her heart and wanted me to be happy, but she wasn't too keen on the idea of a dog in the house. With animals came messes, and she didn't have time to do extra cleaning or take care of a pet. Every time I asked, she answered, "No! No! No!"

But I kept at it, and she began to soften. Why, I wasn't sure. (Later I found out that she was worried about my loneliness. Her tender heart could see how much I needed something to love.)

She told me I could have a tiny dog, between eight and ten pounds. I was so excited that I immediately crawled upstairs to begin researching dog breeds on the Internet with Caitlin.

A few days later, I sat down with my mom to go over my research. The first words out of my mouth were, "Mom, I've found the perfect dog breed for me!"

"Oh?"

"Yes," I said. "I want a dog that's low-key, one that will lie around and be my best friend." A porch dog.

"That sounds good."

"The one I want has long, droopy ears and a sad face. I know all about the temperament of this breed." I filled her in on all the details about coonhounds, the kind of dog I'd chosen. But I paused when I got to the part she wouldn't like. "There's one problem."

"What's the problem, Gabe?"

I held my breath. If she said that two-letter word, my heart would break.

"When these dogs are full grown," I said, "they get over sixty pounds."

"No. No way. There is no way we are having a dog that large in the house, Gabe! It will never happen!" She turned and walked away.

ALL ABOUT
COONHOUNDS

Coonhounds were bred to chase and tree prey such as raccoons. (To "tree" an animal means chasing it up a tree so that human hunters can catch it.) They have an excellent sense of smell and are good trackers. But don't let them off the leash unless they're very well trained—that sense of smell can lead them far astray if they find an interesting track to follow! Coonhounds are smart, gentle dogs, loyal to their family and pack.

Height: twenty-three to twenty-seven inches

Weight: generally between sixty to one hundred pounds

Appearance: short, sleek black coat with tan markings; long muzzle and long ears

Sources:
http://abtcc.com;
http://www.akc.org/breeds/black_tan_coonhound/index.cfm
"coonhound"; *Encyclopedia Britannica.* Encyclopedia Britannica Deluxe Edition. Chicago: Encyclopedia Britannica, 2010; http://www.dogbreedinfo.com/blackandtancoonhound.htm

I had gotten this far, and I couldn't let it go. I pestered her for weeks, trying to convince her that a coonhound was perfect. "Mom, I love their faces and their long, droopy ears," I begged. Eventually, I got up the nerve to ask, "Just do me a favor, Mom. Call the breeder I found online and ask her about puppies. I want a little girl dog, one with the longest ears possible."

Mom still wasn't happy, but she picked up the phone. I hovered the whole time she was on the phone with the breeder, listening and interrupting. "What's she saying, Mom? Ask her if she has a girl, one with long ears."

"Let me talk, Gabe. Let me talk. I'll tell you in a minute."

When Mom told the breeder that she'd give it some thought and get back to her, my heart raced. There was a chance!

Mom hung up the phone. "Chris Hooker does happen to have a female puppy available," she said. "And she happens to have the longest ears in the litter." As if that wasn't enough, she added, "This puppy's temperament is very mellow."

What more could I want? Somehow I knew in my heart this puppy was predestined to be mine.

Of course, Mom hadn't actually said yes yet.

And besides, there was Rick, plus Papa. Caitlin was on my side. She knew the dog would be good for me. I wondered what my mima would have thought. I bet she would have been happy for me and would have wanted me to have this puppy.

My papa just rolled his eyes and shook his head. But Rick quickly said, "No way!"

It was Mom, actually, who talked him into it. This was the first time she'd seen a deep passion inside of me about anything since I'd had to give up dance. The excitement in my eyes and my enthusiasm about caring for a dog pushed her into agreeing to something she'd never thought she'd do. And even into convincing Rick that a big dog would be worth it.

Owning a dog would do a lot for me, she told Rick. It would give me meaning and a purpose in my life, something I hadn't had in years. Taking care of a dog would mean I'd have a real reason to get up in the morning. Mom assured Rick that every responsibility for this dog would be on my shoulders. It took a while, but Rick finally agreed.

And Mom told me the conditions.

"Just like you're my daughter, this dog will be your little girl," Mom told me. "You'll be physically and financially responsible for her. When the puppy has to go to the vet for anything, I'll drive you, but you have to take her in and do all the talking." I felt like I could do this. After all, it would probably only be once a year for her annual visit.

Mom went on. "Even if the puppy has to go outside in the middle of the night, you'll have to crawl to the back door and let her out yourself, Gabe." She wasn't trying to be mean—she knew that I needed to get out of the house and talk to people more than I had been doing. Plus, the exercise I'd get by taking care of a puppy on my own would keep my muscles strong.

But the breeder didn't yet know anything about my ataxia. When Mom called back, she told Chris about my disease. She wanted to be sure the puppy wouldn't be too big and strong for me once she was full grown.

"No, this dog is mellow," Chris assured her. "She'll be fine."

Mom hung up and told me, "The female puppy with the longest ears in the litter will be yours, Gabe."

I was stoked.

Just like a mother getting ready for a newborn baby, I got ready for my new puppy. I bought everything she'd need: toys, leashes, puppy shampoo, toothbrush, and paste. I even had a towel with her name stitched on it.

But there was one thing my dog would need that I hadn't counted on.

A day or so after my mom's second conversation with Chris, the phone rang again. I answered it, and there was the breeder on the other end of the line. Chris was curious about something. Was I already using a wheelchair?

"I can't let the puppy come to your house unless there's a wheelchair in it, Gabe," she told me. "Puppies need to grow up around wheels, or they could become fearful of them. When the puppy is bigger, I don't want her to be afraid to walk beside you." Chris was very conscientious about who she would let her puppies go live with, and she clearly wanted to be sure that this one would be able to adjust to everything her new life would bring her.

Still, the thought of getting a wheelchair made me want to vomit. I'd known deep down inside since I was thirteen that one day I'd end up using one. Even so, I was determined to push that day away for as long as I could.

But I was willing to do anything—even buy

a wheelchair—to make this puppy mine.

So I gave in. I'd accept a wheelchair in the house. But I hadn't agreed to cooperate in buying one. The day came to visit a store and place an order, and my mood was dark. The saleswoman tried to get me to look over the catalog. What did I want? That was the problem. I didn't want a wheelchair at all. I didn't want to have one or need one any more than I'd wanted Friedreich's ataxia in the first place.

I couldn't even bring myself to look at the saleswoman, let alone listen to what she had to say. To her a wheelchair was a tool that would help me get around. To me, it was a banner that announced, "Look at me! I'm disabled!"

We placed the order as quickly as we could and left.

When the wheelchair arrived, it sat folded up in our dining room. I threw a blanket over it so I wouldn't have to look at it.

The wheelchair was for the puppy, not for me. I'd agreed to buy it and had even gone to the store. But I'd never said I would use it. I couldn't even bear to say the word *wheelchair*.

We could go shopping, my mom said. Or to lunch. Or to a movie. We could go anywhere now that we had the chair. Mom insisted that she wasn't trying to take away my independence but give me more.

Still, I refused, over and over. I'd go along on errands, using Mom as my walker to reach the car. But I wouldn't get out and walk through a store—I didn't want anyone to see me fall—and I wouldn't use the wheelchair.

I could still walk at home as long as I was holding on to something. I wasn't going to give that up. In fact, I had started in-home physical therapy to help me keep my strength, which would help me with my dog. But as far as I was concerned, sitting in a wheelchair meant defeat. It meant giving up forever on controlling my own body. It meant going out in public as a disabled person, a target for staring eyes and mocking laughter.

I couldn't do that. I just couldn't. Not even for my very own dog.

About a month before my puppy was due to arrive, Chris called to ask me a question. My puppy needed a name so that she could be registered as a purebred at the American Kennel Club.

The first part of my dog's name would have to be "Foxfire"; that was Chris's co-breeder Bob Urban's kennel, and all his dogs carried that name. (Chris owned Izzy's father, Bruce, and Izzy's mother, Faye, was from Bob's kennel.) Then I'd have to get creative. Registered names can only have so many characters, and the American Kennel Club limits the number of dogs that can have the same name. And Chris wanted all the dogs in this litter to be named after song titles. "I don't care if it's a country song, rock and roll, religious, or whatever, but let me know what you come up with," she told me.

For a couple of weeks I listened intently to songs on the radio. "Building a Mystery" by Sarah McLachlan was popular, and it didn't take me long to decide that Foxfire Building a Mystery would be my dog's name.

But she also needed a call name, one to use every day. I could have called her "Sarah," but I wanted something more unusual. Eventually, I settled on "Sarah Izabel," Izzy for short.

It was four days before my birthday when we packed up the green van we'd rented for the trip to pick up my new dog. What a present my Izzy would be! Bob was planning to meet us in Ohio with the puppy.

We knew the minute Bob arrived, because when he pulled into the hotel parking lot, we could hear the dogs and puppies whining inside his SUV.

Bob came in and introduced himself. I was glad to meet him, but my heart wasn't in making small talk. All I could think about was Izzy. I could hardly wait to meet her. What would it be like to finally hold my puppy?

We went out to peek in the back of Bob's truck, and then Bob suggested we go back inside. He would bring Izzy to me.

I sat in a chair in a hotel room, waiting anxiously. At last Bob came in. Gently, he placed my little girl into my arms.

My heart instantly overflowed. Her ears were perfect—long and velvety. The size of her paws amazed me. They were huge, compared to the rest of her! Her belly was warm and soft. Holding her to my face, I kissed her on the top of her head. How could I resist?

She was finally mine.

When I put her on the floor and watched her walk, her tiny tail stuck straight up, and I noticed the cute little brown patch on her bottom. We gave her water from the pink bowl Chris had given us, and she drained the bowl and carried it around in her mouth, as if asking for a refill. Adorable.

My mom, my sister, and I played with Izzy on the bed for a while until we noticed how late it had gotten. We had to get on the road. Bob gave me some verbal instructions on how to feed and care for her. He also gave me his phone number in case I had questions after we arrived home. I hated to put my little puppy in her crate, but as Bob told me, it was the safest way for her to travel.

Izzy didn't know that, however, and about half an hour into the trip, she started crying. We talked to her, but she wouldn't settle down. When we couldn't stand it any longer, Mom pulled over and went to take her from the crate. The moment Izzy was on my lap, she stopped her whimpering. I was amazed; we'd bonded so quickly.

Mom couldn't resist reaching over and rubbing the puppy's soft feet. "Are you sure this is the dog you want?" she asked. "If she's not, we can turn around and take her back."

I didn't realize she was teasing. "Oh, no," I said instantly. "This is the perfect dog for me."

Once we reached home, it took a while for us to settle into a routine. But I loved Izzy like a mom, and I was willing to do anything for her, even sliding off my bed and crawling outside with her in the middle of the night if she needed to go. My mom had told me that's what I'd need to do, and I did it.

Soon I began to notice something about Izzy—something that wasn't quite right.

The weather was warm for early spring, so Mom and I sat on the back porch while Izzy played with Madeline and Caitlin. I couldn't run with my puppy, but I loved watching her romp with my sisters. Izzy didn't seem to have much energy, I noticed. Before long she'd find her way back to the mattress on the porch and settle down for a nap.

At first I didn't think too much about it. But then a car backfired so loudly it made us all jump. Izzy didn't even budge, and I began to think something wasn't right. Mom noticed, too. "Mom, what's wrong with Izzy?" I asked. "Is my little girl deaf?"

Mom tried to wake Izzy, but the puppy slept on. I asked her to call Chris. But Chris wasn't too worried. Izzy had been through many changes, she reminded me, and puppies do sleep a lot during the day. I let myself feel reassured. Izzy was fine.

I didn't know it, but this was only the first of many moments that meant Izzy would really live up to her registered name: Foxfire Building a Mystery.

Chapter Seven

DISNEY

That first night with Izzy when Mom checked up on her three girls snuggling with my new puppy, she glanced at the snow globe I kept on my dresser. Mom had bought it for me as a gift because I loved the Pirates of the Caribbean ride at Disney World when I was four. Goofy was inside, dressed as a pirate, and when Mom turned the key in the base, the song "Yo Ho! (A Pirate's Life for Me)" broke the silence. The song set a whirlwind of joyful memories going in her mind, and it also sparked an idea. We would take a family vacation to Disney World.

A trip I would not be going on.

There was no way I could walk around a huge amusement park hanging on to my mom—I could barely make it to our vehicle. I'd need to use a wheelchair. And that was something I was still not willing to do.

Mom was on a mission. She sent away for theme park pamphlets and a Disney video. My little sisters watched the video. I didn't. Still, I could hear the songs through my bedroom walls. "Yo ho, yo ho, a pirate's life for me!" I loved that song. I loved Goofy. He looked like a coonhound, like Izzy with her long, droopy ears.

Madeline and Caitlin talked about nothing but Disney—the trip, the rides, the sights. And Mom didn't give up. It'll be fun, Gabe. You'll love it, Gabe. We'll all be together. She reminded me that nobody knew me in Florida, so why would it matter if people saw me in the chair? She didn't ask for an answer right away; she just asked me to think about it.

And Mom had one last trick up her sleeve. If we drove to Florida, we could stop in North Carolina and visit Chris Hooker, Izzy's breeder. There, I could meet Izzy's dad, Bruce, her mother, Faye, and her brother, Ben. Now I was intrigued. I already loved Izzy. I couldn't miss meeting her furry family.

GABE'S EARLY YEARS

Gabe as a young dancer

Ready for the stage!

Young Gabe with a
feline friend—always
an animal lover!

FROM THE FAMILY ALBUM

*Feeling the effects
of bullying*

*Senior year: still
walking without help*

*A mother's love
never dies.*

With her favorite character—Goofy—at Disneyland

Disney princesses

With her sisters Madeline (l) and Caitlin (r) and Minnie Mouse

IZZY JOINS THE FAMILY

Izzy's mother, Faye, with her litter

Izzy as a young puppy

Gabe meets her "daughter," Izzy

Izzy waiting to go to her new home

"Grandma" Hooker

TRAVELS WITH IZZY

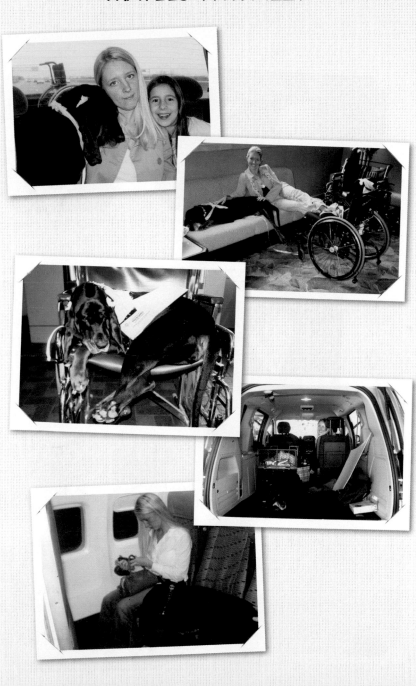

GETTING OUR ANTI-BULLYING MESSAGE OUT

Animal Planet's A Pet Story

Speaking to groups

CONNECTING WITH STUDENTS

REMEMBERING AND LOOKING AHEAD

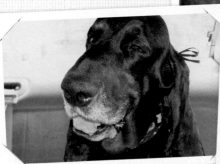

Remembering Izzy

Gabe with ILO,
"Izzy Lives On"

Living life to the fullest!

I finally told Mom I would go.

I hated leaving Izzy at the kennel, but Mom promised that she'd be all right and that the people at the kennel were kind. When they said I could call and check up on her, I breathed a huge sigh of relief. The nineteen-hour journey seemed to take forever, but when we saw the Disney World sign, it was already worth it.

Disney World was everything I remembered, and then some. I went on most of the rides; my favorite was still Pirates of the Caribbean. I didn't like the idea of letting people see me in my chair, but to my surprise, it was fine. Nobody made fun of me, nobody judged me. It was so different from life at school. It felt magical.

Unfortunately, SeaWorld was a different story.

Caitlin, Rick, and I waited in line for the water coaster ride, Journey to Atlantis. There was a separate entrance for people in wheelchairs, and I asked an attendant where I should go. She seemed annoyed. Did she think I was being a nuisance on purpose? She even rolled her eyes at me. Would she have done that if I weren't in a wheelchair? I wheeled myself back to where Mom waited for us at the exit. She could tell I was upset, but she was still hoping we could all have fun. Don't let this

HOW TO TREAT SOMEONE WITH A DISABILITY

Do you know someone who uses a wheelchair or a walker, or who can't hear or see well, or who has trouble talking? Maybe you're not quite sure how to act around this person. Here are some ideas to keep in mind:

- Say hi. Smile. Make eye contact. You'd be surprised how many people refuse to do this, and how lonely it can feel.

- Include. Don't assume that a disabled person won't be able to do what you're doing, or wouldn't want to try.

- It's okay to ask politely about an illness or a disability. But a disabled person may not want to discuss it. If someone says, "Sorry, that's private," or "I don't want to talk about that," you need to respect that answer.

- Ask before you offer help. A disabled person might want to do something for himself—even if it takes longer. And don't be offended if they say no—just know you did a good thing by asking, and feel good about yourself!

- If you can't understand what someone with a speech problem says, it's okay to ask her to repeat it. Or to repeat it yourself and let her tell you if you got it right. But wait for her to finish talking, and don't interrupt or try to finish a sentence.

- If you're talking to someone in a wheelchair, get down to that level or pull up a chair.

- Don't pet or play with a service dog unless you ask. The dog has a job, and you might distract it without meaning to.

- If you see people teasing, mocking, imitating, pushing, tripping, or otherwise bullying someone with a disability, speak up! Tell them to stop or get an adult to help.

- Always remember that a disability is a very small part of who a person is. Mostly, you're looking at someone very similar to you.

Sources:
http://www.girlshealth.gov/disability/know/treat.cfm
http://www.dol.gov/odep/pubs/fact/comucate.htm

one incident ruin your day, Gabe, she coaxed. Just blow it off and forget her.

Forget what had happened? Forget that I was in a wheelchair, the last place I ever wanted to be? My tears quickly turned to sobs. People gawked. I hated being stared at, and crying was just making it worse, but I couldn't calm down. A girl even asked me if I was faking my disability so I could get on rides faster. Was this what being in a wheelchair would always be like? If so, I wanted no part of it.

Caitlin was exasperated. Another family outing was about to fall apart because of me. Mom stepped in. "The Shamu show is about to start. Let's head that way."

The Shamu show? I'd have to sit in a special section for wheelchairs, away from my family. No, thank you.

"Okay." Mom wasn't about to let the vacation be ruined for everybody. "If you don't want to go and you can't shrug this off, meet the rest of us at the park exit at five o'clock. I'm not going to let this day be ruined for Caitlin and Madeline."

Mom had always told me that she would not disable me more than my condition already had. She'd always treated me like any other kid. Still,

I was surprised. Were they really going to walk away from me? Madeline, only four years old, was worried about me, but Mom was firm. In a few minutes, they were gone.

I wasn't really used to the wheelchair yet, and it was hard to get around. So I mostly sat. My nose and the skin of my legs started to burn in the sun, and a lady came up and offered me some sunscreen. I sat some more, and people watched, and I thought.

Rick and Mom had spent a lot of money on the SeaWorld tickets, and I'd been about to let my anger spoil the day for everyone. It hadn't been fair, the way that lady had treated me. But that didn't give me the right to ruin everybody else's fun.

A five o'clock, I rolled up to the gate where Mom had said we would meet, and I saw my family coming. I began to smile.

"Are you sorry you spent the day alone, Gabe?" Mom asked.

"Yes!"

I knew it hadn't been easy for her, either, to walk away and leave me alone. But she'd done it. And I'd learned something valuable. I was going to have to figure out how to shake off the things that bothered me, if I were going to survive in my new world—a wheelchair world. I would have to become a stronger person, but it would take me time.

I'd already known that my mom would never give up on me. Now I learned that she would draw a line and stick to it. She would help me only if I helped myself.

It was a lot to take in. I was glad to get back to the hotel and rest, and think about seeing my Izzy soon. But first I was going to meet her family.

Chapter Eight

ANOTHER DIAGNOSIS

Shortly after we arrived in North Carolina, Chris handed me a new mulberry-colored collar. "It's for Izzy from her Grandma Hooker," she said with a grin.

Grandma Hooker was only one of Izzy's relatives that we were about to meet.

Izzy got her long body and short legs from her mother, Faye, but she looked more like her father, Bruce, in the face. He was top coonhound, and didn't think twice about barking at the other dogs to keep them in line. Faye was mellow and sweet. And Izzy's brother, Ben, was huge! He loved to snuggle; in fact, he thought he was a lapdog. Not quite! Bruce had loads of energy, too, and a playfulness that surprised me. Izzy was so much quieter.

As much as I enjoyed the trip, I couldn't wait to get to the kennel and pick up my Izzy girl. Her long ears swung back and forth as she trotted over to lick my face, and she lay down beside me right away so that I could rub her belly.

"How was she?" Mom asked one of the workers at the kennel.

"Not very active," was the reply.

"What do you mean?"

"Izzy doesn't have the energy most young puppies do," the woman told us. "We were wondering if maybe you don't socialize her enough. She just didn't want to play with the other dogs, and she wanted nothing to do with going for walks. She only wanted to sleep. That's really not normal. You need to make sure she's spending enough time with people and other dogs, or you're not going to have a very happy dog."

Did they think I didn't take good care of Izzy?

At home, Rick helped me give Izzy a bath. She was dirty and had sores on her elbows from sleeping on the kennel's rough cement floor. Even her shiny, velvety coat had gone dull. It broke my heart to see her like this. Mom and I agreed that we'd never put her in a kennel again.

Still, I was bothered by what the woman at the kennel had said. Could something be wrong with Izzy?

We took Izzy to see our veterinarian, Dr. Sandy Smith, who gave us some medication for her elbows but said she seemed fine otherwise.

Fine? Not really. That evening I watched Izzy, restless in her crate. She turned and turned in circles and pressed her head against the side of the crate, as if she couldn't get comfortable. She vomited the next day and seemed to want to do nothing but sleep.

We called Chris, but she wasn't worried. Puppies do sleep a lot, she reminded us. Maybe Izzy had eaten something that had upset her stomach.

We wanted the answer to be that simple and decided to give Izzy a few days to see if she'd get better. But Izzy had other ideas.

That night, Mom and Rick left for dinner and a movie. I was alone with Izzy, and she suddenly began to retch and struggle, as if she were choking. I thought her collar must be too tight, and cut it off with a pair of scissors. Then I called Mom to explain what was happening. She and Rick came right home.

We sat together in the kitchen, watching Izzy. One minute she would seem fine, and the next she was restless, coughing, or getting up to stagger into walls. Then, exhausted, she'd collapse into her crate and sleep. I lay on the hardwood floor beside her for the entire night.

When I woke, early the next morning, I yelled, "Mom!"

She and Rick flew down the stairs. Izzy lay limp and helpless in her crate. She was unable to move or even to stand. She was in trouble.

We brought her in to see Dr. Sandy right away. X-rays showed that Izzy *had* eaten something, just as Chris had suspected—a rock! Not a small one, either. She'd need surgery right away.

I went home and worried until Dr. Sandy called. The surgery was over, she said, but Izzy wasn't coming out of the anesthetic as quickly as she should. Would I come in? She thought the sound of my voice and the touch of my hands might help wake Izzy up.

I got there as quickly as I could. As I talked to Izzy, I rubbed my fingers down her long, velvety ears. And before long, Izzy opened her eyes.

As Dr. Sandy was telling me about how to care for Izzy, she mentioned something else. She suspected Izzy might have a liver shunt.

I didn't know what a liver shunt was, but at just the sound of the words, my heart beat ten times faster.

Why my dog, why my dog, why my dog?

Dr. Sandy was right. Izzy did indeed have a liver shunt. When blood flows through the liver, toxins and anything that could harm the body are filtered out. In Izzy's case, some of the unfiltered blood was escaping back into her arteries and veins, carrying the toxins all over her body. When toxins build up in the brain, they can cause symptoms. And that's what we started to see, more and more, in Izzy.

She stumbled. She staggered. She bumped into walls. She couldn't count on her body to do what she wanted it to. Things that were easy for other young dogs—walking, running, chasing, playing—got harder and harder for her.

This was all very familiar. Izzy looked a lot like me.

Izzy would need another surgery, and soon, to correct the liver shunt. When I'd told Mom I wanted a dog, I'd agreed to pay for everything she needed. But I'd never expected my dog to need major surgery—and more than once. Plus regular exams afterward to keep track of her condition.

I didn't have a job; I'd never actually gotten work

as a travel agent. Maybe I could have managed it, but I have to admit—I wasn't willing to try. Working a job meant I'd have to interact with people every day, people who would see me as disabled. Mom couldn't be at my side at work, acting as a walker, or carry me piggyback back and forth every day from her car. Without my mom to help, I'd have to use a wheelchair. The thought of being seen in a chair made me panic inside. More than panic—it terrified me. I couldn't face the fear. No wheelchair, no matter what. Florida was one thing, but here in my hometown where former classmates might see me was another story.

So, no job. I got a disability check every month. Everything Izzy needed had to come from that.

I managed to pay Dr. Sandy for the first surgery, and she let me set up a payment plan for all of the tests Izzy needed. But she couldn't perform the liver shunt surgery. We needed to find a surgeon somewhere who'd let me pay a bit at a time.

If I didn't find some way to pay for the surgery, my little girl would die. I couldn't let that happen.

Izzy was like my own daughter. My mom would never give up on me, and I was not about to give up on my dog. She had brought joy to my life, the first joy I'd felt in a long time. She was my reason for getting up in the morning, something to care about and to care for. She was why I lived and breathed. I was not about to let her down.

My mom called my uncle to ask for his advice. He suggested a fund-raiser.

"A fund-raiser!" Mom exclaimed. "Absolutely not! No way! Gabe does not take charity!"

Mom reminded my uncle that I had agreed to be responsible for whatever Izzy needed. Now, I'd already done all I could, and my mom had helped as much as she was able. Mom was willing to admit that we might need some assistance from family at this point. But not from strangers!

My mom has always liked being the one to give, not the one to take. But my uncle Clayton told her she'd have to swallow her pride. This wasn't about her; it was about my needing help for my dog. Mom finally agreed.

As for me, I'd do anything for Izzy. If that meant a fund-raiser, I was all for it!

My uncle talked to a friend, Kim, and asked if Kim could come and visit Izzy and me. Mom agreed, thinking this would be just about the fund-raiser. It turned out to be something different. Kim wanted to interview me for the *Flint Journal* newspaper.

He wanted to do something else, too. He wanted to take a picture of Izzy and me.

A picture of me in my wheelchair.

I hated the whole idea. After all those years of pretending nothing was wrong with me, doing everything I could to look normal—how could I stand to have a picture of me in a wheelchair, right there in the paper for everyone in town to see? I hadn't even let anyone take a picture of me in the wheelchair at Disney.

But this wasn't about me. Izzy was sick. She was going to die. I'd said I would do anything to help her—even this.

I let him take the photograph.

Kim's story was called "Gabe and Izzy Lean on Each Other to Survive Tragic Disease." Alongside the article, there was the picture. I was sitting in my chair, and Izzy had jumped up to put her paws around my neck. She looked so sweet—but me? I looked like a person in a wheelchair, exactly what I'd never wanted to be.

When Mom held the paper up to show me the article, I turned my face away.

An old friend of Mom's called when she saw the article and volunteered to organize a fundraiser for Izzy. Mom had to be talked into it. But her friend didn't take no for an answer. People like to help, she told Mom, if they're allowed to. And Mom reluctantly agreed.

Fund-raising canisters went up all over town, at banks, vets' offices, everywhere. My name was on them, and Izzy's, too, and the newspaper photo of me hugging Izzy was right on the front. The idea of letting people see me like that—it was scary. Suppose some of the kids who'd tormented me in high school walked by one of those canisters and saw the picture? But I found the courage to accept it, because I hoped it would help Izzy.

And it did.

The cans had slots so that people could drop donations inside: coins, dollars, whatever they wanted. One man made a donation of one thousand dollars! An elementary school took up a collection. A Girl Scout troop sent a contribution along with a card all the girls had signed. Some people in town brought dog food for Izzy; some sent flowers. As soon as the money came in, I'd drop it off at Dr. Sandy's office to pay off what I owed.

I was still frightened of letting anyone outside my family see me as being disabled. But as the donations came in, week after week, I began to see that people in my town weren't judging me or mocking me when they found out I had ataxia. Instead they were actually coming together to take care of Izzy—and of me.

I was astounded.

Dr. Sandy's vet bills were paid. Relieved, I started sleeping better. But Izzy still needed the second surgery. A friend of a friend (who owned Izzy's sister) helped us out and found a vet who offered to do Izzy's surgery for free.

"Absolutely not!" Mom didn't like the idea. "We're not looking for the surgery to be donated, just a payment plan for Gabe."

But the vet insisted. He would not do the surgery unless we accepted it as a donation. And there would still be bills for X-rays, medicines, and the stay at the clinic for Izzy. We'd have a chance to pay our share.

And I'd have a chance to fight for my little girl.

No matter how tough it was, I had to take care of Izzy. I had promised.

It was scary for me to talk to strangers, but I did it for Izzy. I called vets, made appointments, and asked what I needed to do to take care of my dog.

It was a struggle for me simply to get out of the

house, but I did it for Izzy. My mom would hold me up as we walked to the car on one of our many trips to the vet. If I fell, she promised, it would be on top of her. She'd be the one to get hurt, not me. There were a few times I thought we'd hit the pavement, but she never let me go, and we always got Izzy to her appointments.

It felt humiliating to me when my mom would pull the car into a handicapped space. The first time she got a handicapped parking permit, I tore it up. But Mom got another and told me that if I hid or ruined the second one, I'd owe her fifty dollars for the time she'd spend replacing it. I didn't tear up the second sticker. I knew that Izzy couldn't walk far; she needed to be close to the vet's building. I left that sticker on the windshield, where everyone else could see it. I did it for Izzy.

I even faced my worst fear and let myself be seen in a wheelchair. First there were the pictures in the newspaper and on the fund-raising canisters. And then there was Izzy's surgeon. When we had an appointment at that office, I didn't have any choice; I had to use the chair. It was the only way I could cover the distance from the parking lot to the building. So I got out of the car, into the chair, and I wheeled myself inside. It wasn't something I would have done for myself. But I did it for Izzy.

As always, Izzy was a mystery. The second surgery couldn't locate her shunt; it must have been invisible, deep inside her liver. But cutting her liver open meant she'd only have a fifty-fifty chance of survival.

I didn't want her dying on the table. "Bring her back home!" I said.

We tried adjusting her diet, since her liver couldn't handle protein. A special prescription dog food worked wonders. And Izzy worked wonders for me.

As I got out in the world to take care of Izzy, my fear of being seen by the people who'd once made fun of me slowly began to fade. The bullies from my past were no longer running my life.

My loneliness eased up, too. The staff and vets I had to talk to for Izzy's sake became friends. I met many wonderful people who showed me they cared about Izzy and about me. This wasn't like my days at school. People were kind, and caring, and helpful.

Not long after Izzy's recovery from her second surgery, I decided to get a professional photo taken of the two of us together. When we arrived at the studio, there was a picture on the wall of a little girl wearing a pair of angel wings.

It was perfect.

Mom has always called my dog "Angel Izzy." She believes Izzy was meant for me. So I put the wings on Izzy for the photograph.

Mom was right—Izzy was an angel for me.

Chapter Nine

ANIMAL PLANET

"I. Will. Not. Do. It." I made every word into its own sentence.

Mom threw up her hands and stormed out of the room.

She had every right to be upset with me. The crew from Animal Planet was scheduled to film in two days, and I was a mess.

Animal Planet had contacted me about my relationship with Izzy. Someone from the network had seen an article about me and wanted to film a piece about the two of us for the show *A Pet Story*. A girl and a dog, both fighting disabling disease, depending on each other to survive—it would be great TV.

At first I'd agreed. I'd had my beloved Izzy a year, and I could not and would not deny how much she had changed my life.

Izzy was my furry girl, my four-legged daughter. I promised to take care of her as a mother would her child. But the truth was that, all this time, Izzy was actually the one caring for me. She took my mind off my own illness and my worries about being seen as disabled. My life became about her, not about me. Taking care of Izzy forced me out of my self-made prison.

But could I truly do this for her? How could I talk about my disease on national television when I couldn't talk to my own family about it? I didn't even know much about Friedreich's ataxia, because I'd refused to learn. I had myself convinced that even talking about my condition would make me depressed. But the truth was, I'd erupt in rage if anybody brought it up. I'd retreat to my bedroom and slam the door.

Now I curled up on my bed in a fetal position, something I hadn't done since the days before I'd gotten Izzy. True, I'd spoken to a few newspaper reporters about my relationship with my dog, but this was different. It was TV. People would see the way I walked, and people would hear the way I talked. Would there be millions of people, all over the country, laughing at me, instead of just a bunch of hometown kids who bully?

But if I backed out now, I'd be letting everybody down.

I'd talked to the producer, Joe Zimmerman. He had a real gift for putting me at ease. He promised me that the filming would be fun. Maybe he was right. And I'd always liked Animal Planet.

But still—could I actually do it? Let people see me this way on national television?

I couldn't sleep. And I couldn't make up my mind. I tossed and turned, trying to think. And little by little I saw this for what it actually was—a great honor. I'd appear on a network I had always loved and watched every chance I got. And more than anything, I owed this to Izzy. I was healing on the inside because of her, and I couldn't hide in my room and refuse to tell everybody about the love we shared.

And Joe was right. The taping turned out to be a lot of fun, for me and for my family, too. The crew—Joe, the cameraman, and the sound engineer—spent four days with us and blended right in with our family. They made jokes, teased, and laughed with us. Joe found out that I was a tap-dancing duck in my first dance recital and sang, "Rubber Ducky, You're the One" to me. How could I keep myself from cracking up? On day two, when we had lunch with the crew at Applebee's, Joe took my mom's place, helping me walk into the restaurant with an arm around my waist. Another day he stopped the filming to help Mom sew straps on Caitlin's ballet shoes. He seemed like just a part of the family.

They filmed every aspect of my life and Izzy's, interviewing her vet, my doctors, and even doing a segment at the mall where I used to enjoy shopping. On the first day, they followed my morning routine with Izzy, and filmed me brushing my hair and choosing one of my many shades of lipstick. Having a camera in my face while I did these little things made me nervous. I was sure I'd drop my mascara or my hairbrush; I have trouble holding on to things sometimes, a symptom of ataxia. Fortunately, that day, everything went smoothly.

It wasn't so smooth when the camera crew followed me for a visit with Izzy's wonderful vet, Dr. Sandy. Izzy and I were a lot alike—she didn't like going to the doctor any more than I did. But

I couldn't run away from my doctor's appointments. Izzy could. She might have been slow, but she knew where she didn't want to go! Once we were out of the van and Izzy realized where she was, she bolted as fast as she could manage toward the road, with five-year-old Madeline clinging to her leash.

On the last day, Joe interviewed me in depth, at home. This time he wasn't just asking me to talk about Izzy. He was asking about me. I didn't get too specific when I told him about my school days, but even so I had to hold back tears. I didn't want anyone feeling sorry for me, though, and I said as much on camera. I never had. I didn't want to be picked on or to be pitied—I just wanted to be me, Gabe.

When the filming was over at last and the crew was ready to leave, we traded gifts. Joe gave me an Animal Planet sweatshirt, which I wore until it fell apart, and a three-pound box of chocolates; he knew how much I loved them. I gave everybody in the crew a copy of the Disney movie *The Duke*. The dog in the movie happens to be related to Izzy. It's kind of funny, but Izzy comes from a line of celebrities. I think she was born to be stellar!

I couldn't bear to say good-bye. I just said, "See you later." Good-byes are too final, and too painful, for me. I haven't seen Joe and the rest of the crew since, but I know someday I will.

"Izzy and Gabe" aired first in April of 2001. By 2005, it had aired more than eighty-five times, one of the most popular episodes of *A Pet Story* ever produced. I've never watched it. I just don't like the way my voice sounds; I don't want to listen to it on TV. And I still can't bear to hear too much about Friedreich's ataxia: how the symptoms get worse, how many people die. I knew they'd discuss that on the show, and I just don't want to know.

Other people watched it, though. Lots of them. And letters began pouring in. People were touched by my story, and Izzy's, and they wanted to tell us so.

Dear Gabe,

I happened to catch your show in 2003 when I was recovering in the hospital from my seventh surgery to repair a hernia surgery that had gone wrong. The courage and determination that you displayed, as well as your statement that you don't want anybody to feel sorry for you, gave me the inspiration and strength to get through that time and all of my subsequent surgeries. Thank you so much for what you have done for me.

—Dan Houle

Dear Gabe,

I was hit by a car in a mountain bike accident and not expected to live, never mind walk again. Hearing your story on Animal Planet inspired me to persevere. Not only can I walk, but I am now a research scientist.

Thanks for your willingness to share your incredible story.

—Sean Nasri

I kept the candy box that Joe had given me for years and carefully stored the letters I received in it—a constant reminder of that special time in my life.

Chapter Ten

BACK TO SCHOOL

I can't imagine how many people saw me and Izzy on Animal Planet. But that still didn't mean I felt comfortable or confident about going out into the world. When my little sister Madeline was invited to a birthday party at Chuck E. Cheese's, Mom had to prod me to go along.

When I finally agreed, I thought I'd stay in the car. I used my normal excuse—I didn't want to run into any of the kids I used to know at school. Mom was quick to point out that the restaurant wasn't in our neighborhood, and that nobody would know me there except for my friends.

An old family friend, Peggy, the birthday girl's

grandmother, would be there. I gave in. It would be good to see Peggy. And it turned out that Peggy's daughter, Jennifer, was there, too. Jennifer was a teacher at a middle school. In fact, Caitlin was in her class. And she'd been hoping to see me. There was something she wanted to ask.

Would I be willing to come to her school and talk to her students about being on Animal Planet?

I hemmed and hawed. After the Animal Planet show had aired, I'd been asked to speak at a couple of elementary schools. At first I'd been nervous, but the little kids were welcoming and sweet. They made posters for Izzy and me. Some raised money for Izzy's vet bills. And mostly they wanted to ask questions about Izzy, not me. I loved it!

But middle school? That was different.

The worst time of my life had started in eighth grade. I'd had kids mocking the way I talked, laughing when I fell. I'd had spit wads sticking to my face and landing in my hair. I'd been punched and shoved and threatened. And I'd heard those cruel words, over and over. "What's wrong with you, Gabe?" "Are you drunk, Gabe?" "Got a brain tumor, Gabe?"

Still, how could I let Jennifer down? She was a family friend and Caitlin's teacher. Finally,

I said yes. But I wasn't happy about it. Almost immediately, I was sure it had been a mistake. I never should have agreed to walk back into a middle school. The kids would laugh at me, make comments behind my back, and think I was a joke.

Soon all I could think of was: *I have to get out of this. I can't relive those days. I can't do it.*

Still, I couldn't stop time. The day arrived. I was due at Caitlin's school in half an hour.

When I began trembling, Mom noticed and asked what was wrong.

"I can't go back into a school full of eighth graders!" I told her. "The elementary school was one thing, but middle school is another. The memories keep flashing through my head. I feel sick! I keep seeing myself walking down the eighth grade halls. The students are making fun of me. I can't bear to have it happen all over again."

Mom interrupted me. "Gabe, you're not going alone. I'm going to be with you."

I barely heard her. All I could think of was the middle schoolers laughing at me, throwing spit wads and everything else they could get their hands on. My frazzled mind was made up. I was not going. I asked Mom to call Jennifer and cancel.

Mom looked at me. "Did *I* say I would bring my

dog to school and share what it was like being on Animal Planet?"

"No."

"Who did?"

In tears, I admitted it. "I did."

"Then you better do the calling."

I knew Mom thought I wouldn't do it. But I started dialing. "I don't want to go into schools, Mom!" I was about to push the last number when she interrupted me.

"Gabe, think about this! You're due to be at the school in half an hour. If you don't go, the kids are going to be disappointed. They don't care about your disease. They just think it's pretty cool that you and Izzy were on Animal Planet. Gabe, if you confront your fears, they'll go away."

I hesitated. Finally, I changed my mind.

"Okay, stop! I'll do it. But I have three requests."

Mom's expression didn't change. "Okay, let me hear them."

"First, I don't want to go in the front door of the school."

"No problem."

"Second, I don't want to be seen in the hallways between classes."

"No problem."

"Third, I don't want the students asking me about my disease."

"No problem."

Mom would talk to Jennifer and make sure I'd get what I needed. I knew I wasn't making this easy, but it was the best I could do.

We left the wheelchair at home. Since we were in a rush after all my hesitation, Mom put Izzy in the car and piggybacked me after her. She never complained when she had to be my walker or carry me. "It's all right," she would say. "I am happy to help you as long as you're trying to help yourself."

I was still shaking in the car, and once we got to the school, my legs began to tremble and my voice quivered so much I was sure the kids would notice. Getting into the building was hard, but Mom held me tight and never let go. A friend came along to hold Izzy's leash.

When we finally arrived at the classroom, Mom knocked at the door. Jennifer opened it. As we stepped inside, my body was trembling as badly as my legs.

At once, all the kids called out to Izzy.

Mom had been right. The kids didn't care about my ataxia. They were just thrilled to meet my dog. Izzy walked slowly through the aisles, stopping at each desk to sniff out any treats the students might give her. Her ears were swinging back and forth and her long tail was hitting the kids. They laughed and petted her as she went by.

There was pizza, popcorn, and soda, and pretty soon the students began asking questions about Animal Planet and about Izzy. What kind of rock had she eaten? What kind of dog was she? What about her liver shunt? That day Izzy was the star, not me. And that was perfect.

No teasing, no names, no pushing, no spit wads. One boy drew a picture of Izzy and me and handed it to me as we left. The day had been nothing like what I'd imagined.

The next time was harder.

I really didn't see myself as a public speaker. I just thought of myself as someone with FA and a wonderful dog who'd visited a couple of schools. I wasn't sure how to handle a request from the National Ataxia Foundation. They asked me to give a talk about Animal Planet and about Izzy, and they also mentioned that a lot of young people with FA have problems with bullying. Maybe my talk could help them.

I was more than a little nervous about the whole idea, and so my uncle Clayton, who was a teacher at a high school in Flint, thought he would help. Why didn't I come and talk to his class about my story? He figured that the more experience I could get talking before a crowd, the better.

His students, though, didn't want to hear about Izzy or Animal Planet. He wanted me to talk to them about what it had been like to be bullied.

That was harder. I'd have Izzy with me, and my sisters had promised to come and bring their dogs as well. (My soft-hearted mom had given in two more times, and each of my sisters now had her own dog, just as I had Izzy.) Having the dogs around, I thought, would take some of the pressure and attention off me.

Not quite.

I waited in the hallway, alone with Izzy and my nerves. I'd almost never talked about the way I had been bullied and how it made me feel. And now? With strangers? But it was too late to back out. I entered the classroom with Izzy at my side, started to speak, and began to cry.

I looked over at Izzy, and it seemed as if she had tears in her eyes as well. The two of us were all alone in front of so many students, and we cried together. Izzy's eyes were fixed on me, and she let out a whimper. For a moment it was as though we were one.

My bond with Izzy was really remarkable, and I believe she could feel my pain. I'd spoken to her many nights, lying on my bedroom floor, telling her my feelings as I ran my fingers down her long ears and stared into her eyes. She always seemed to listen and understand. I think she sensed my sadness that very moment and wanted to comfort me, as I'd done for her after her surgeries.

Izzy did make me feel a little better, and I was able to keep talking through my tears. And Uncle Clayton had been right. Talking openly about being bullied was hard, but having done it once, I could do it again.

When I spoke at the National Ataxia Foundation, I was a little more ready to deal with my feelings, thanks to Uncle Clayton and his students— and, of course, to Izzy. I was brave enough to bring up the way I had been treated in high school. All my listeners could relate. Students with disabilities are more likely to be bullied, and many of them knew exactly what I had been through.

Slowly the word spread about me, and especially about my dog. I'd get a call from one school, then another. I'd go. I'd start to talk about bullying, trying to get the words out and to keep my eyes dry. But someone would ask a question—What did they do to you? What was it like? How did you feel? And years' worth of tears would pour down my face. I had no idea anyone's face could become so saturated from crying.

After being picked on day after day, I'd become an expert at hiding my feelings. But now I was crying in public, letting my pain show. To my surprise, that turned out to be a good thing.

Those tears made a point. The students watching me learned that it's okay to cry, that you don't always have to hide your feelings. And my tears showed them, probably even more than my words, the harm that bullying can do.

Posted by Samantha

You came to my school on Friday, November 30. You are the best and you made the biggest bully in the sixth grade cry. She was so amazed how bullying can impact people's lives so much.

For my listeners really to understand my message, I had to be honest with them. My old motto—if I don't talk about it, I won't have to deal with the pain—had to go. With Izzy by my side, I could tell these kids the truth about bullying, even if that meant I couldn't hold back my tears. When I found the courage to be honest, an amazing thing sometimes happened. Students, sitting in my audience, would start to cry, too.

When I let these teenagers see my feelings, they showed me theirs as well. I was surprised, but I had to admit it to myself—I had a gift to connect with them.

After each presentation ended, we made sure that my listeners could file past me, getting a chance to say hello, pet Izzy, or just smile. Students began hugging me, girls would lay their head on my shoulder and cry. Time after time kids shared with me how they had been bullied. For these students, it's almost as if someone has finally come to save them. Simply to hear someone talking openly about bullying makes them feel they've already been rescued. Many tell me that I've said what they have wanted to say for a long time. After hearing me, they know that they don't have to suffer in silence, the way I did for years.

I just wanted to tell you thank you for coming to our school. I thought you really changed everything around and made my day because when my class left the gym and got back to the classroom they all said they were sorry for all the pain they have caused me by calling me names.

I'll never forget one boy, rather small compared to the others in his class, who kept hanging around after the assembly was over. I could tell he wanted to open up to me.

After the others cleared away, he shared how he gets picked on and made fun of every day, and how tired he was of it. He had felt my pain, and now I felt his. I gave him a Gabe & Izzy "Stand Against Bullying" wristband and a Gabe & Izzy T-shirt that says NOT JUST A BYSTANDER and STANDING UP FOR THE BULLIED on the back, and told him not to blame himself. He saw how I had overcome all of the bullying I'd gone through, how I'd forgiven those who bullied me, and how I'd kept myself from hurting anyone, even myself, while I'd endured what he was enduring. If I'd survived, so could he! I hoped that he had listened closely to the message I had shared earlier about reporting bullying and seeking out someone who would be willing to help. When I was leaving, he opened the door for me and followed me out to the car. "Bye, Gabe, bye, Gabe," he kept yelling. "Thank you so much!"

I can still see his face.

A girl came up to speak to me at a different assembly. She had alopecia, a condition that caused her hair to fall out. Like me, there was something different about her that she simply could not hide. If she wore her wig to school, she was teased. If she didn't wear it, she was teased.

"It doesn't matter that you have this disease," I said. "It's not who you are. You're still beautiful; you're a beautiful person. Don't let what others say get to you." Of course, I know that what others say does hurt, and she knew it, too. "But don't let them have the power and satisfaction," I told her. I didn't want her to do what I had done, and let bullies ruin her life for so long.

It had taken me many years to learn not to let bullies into my mind and my heart. My thoughts are my own, and I can create my own attitude and even find my own joy. No matter how others treat me, I'm not letting those who bullied me steal my joy. I'd done nothing wrong; those who bullied me had. This girl had done nothing wrong, either. I hoped I could help her to see that we shouldn't be the ones to suffer.

After the assembly, she told me, with tears in her brown eyes, that she had heard my message and felt empowered by it. She said that thanks to me she now felt she had the courage to take her wig off and never wear it again. She realized she was not alopecia, any more than I was Freidrich's ataxia!

After speaking at yet another school in Tucson, Arizona, I came home and checked the comments on my online guest book. There was one comment that will stay with me always. A student wrote that he had planned on taking his own life the very same week I'd come to his school. After hearing me talk, he realized that suicide was not the answer. This boy had not been bullied the way I had been. He was dealing with other, very painful things. But as he listened to my story, he realized that there was still something he could look forward to. He found hope.

He gave me credit for saving his life, but he was the one who saved his own life by being open to what I had to say. He thanked me for speaking to his classmates and asked me to continue spreading my message across the United States and across the world. Then he told me I was his true hero.

He was mine, too.

Posted by Anonymous

You recently visited my high school. . . . Your story basically saved my life. Early this week, I was thinking of ending my life. Not due to bullying but because of other reasons. You showed me that life is what you make it and that it can/will get better. You have given me such a hope and a will to see my bright future.

It wasn't just the victims of bullying who let me know they heard and understood what I had to say. My words were also getting through to kids who'd bullied others. Time and time again, kids told me their eyes were opened, their hearts were touched, and they now understood bullying in a way they never had before. Many promised me they would never bully again.

Posted by Chad

I want to thank you for coming to Durand Middle School! I have changed and inspired many of my friends and I saw many of the girls who were so sad for you that they started to cry. You've changed my mind about a lot of things about bullying. I used to bully a few other students and call them names. I wish you and Izzy a happy life together and I thank you for inspiring me.

Just by sharing my story and being open about my feelings, I was changing hundreds of lives. And that change kept working even after Izzy and I left. Students remembered my message and often talked about me years later. Teachers and principals and adults who work in schools tell me that, after I've spoken, they can use my words—along with images of me and Izzy—to remind students how bullying feels and what it can do. They have told me that they like having a face that students can connect with. "What would Gabe and Izzy think?" they ask.

More and more schools asked me to come. It was all by word of mouth. I never tried to promote myself as a speaker; I just let people find me. And they did! People at a school that Izzy and I had visited talked to people at another school, and another, and another. Then the phone would ring, or a message would pop up on e-mail, and we'd have another school on the calendar. All over America, I was in demand!

Being asked to speak, again and again, tells me a lot. The message I'm sending is getting through. Students are starting to consider the impact their words and actions have on one another. They are thinking beyond the moment.

More bookings meant more and more traveling. Travel wasn't easy for me; it meant using the wheelchair, struggling in and out of the car, crawling in and out of hotel bathtubs. It also meant packing Izzy into the car, stopping whenever she needed to stop, finding hotels that would allow dogs.

My mom came with us; she had to, since I could not drive. We drove through snowstorms; we drove all night. One time my poor mom actually fell asleep at the wheel! The car started to drive slower . . . and slower . . . and slower. Thank goodness, a trucker came up behind us and laid on the horn, waking my mom up. She pulled over into a rest stop, and we slept right there in the car.

That wasn't the only time we slept at a rest stop. Or we'd check into a hotel at midnight and get up again at four or five the next morning to be at a school early enough to set up for an assembly.

But it was worth it, for students to hear what I had to say.

My message to these kids is simple: bullying is a choice. A choice no one needs to make. Once students really understand that, they can take actions to make their schools better, safer, kinder places.

In your speech you said to apologize to someone you picked on today because there might not be a tomorrow. Well, guess what? I did. I went up to the girl and had a huge conversation on how sorry I am. She forgave me and now we said "hi" to each other in the hallway. You honestly touched my heart and made me rethink my actions. Tonight, when I say my prayers I am going to include you and Izzy and ask God to help everyone in the world find a way to live and love life just like you. Thank you for everything.

One day a new and interesting request came from Linden Middle School. Instead of asking me to come and talk about Izzy, my disease, or bullying, they asked me to come for a career day. They wanted to encourage the students to start focusing now on what they wanted to do and achieve after high school. There would be 800 middle school students. Izzy and I would be alone in front of all of them.

This time I knew I could do it.

There was so much I could tell them. But I

simply spoke from my heart. It didn't take long before I had their undivided attention. I filled them in on how difficult my school days were. I was even willing to talk about how hard it is to travel in a wheelchair. But I told them that if I could graduate, with all I had to deal with, so could they! They could realize their dreams if they believed in themselves.

During the question-and-answer time, one young boy stood up and said that my presentation was the best his school had ever had. Suddenly he wasn't standing alone. The other 799 students stood up with him! Getting a standing ovation from 800 kids was something I will never forget. It was incredible—not because I was looking for praise or applause, but because these were middle school students, the ones I had feared most.

It seemed I had nothing to be afraid of anymore. If I could get through to 800 middle school students, maybe I'd finally found my purpose in life. Or maybe I should say my purpose found me.

Chapter Eleven

TWO OF A KIND

Our whole family had decided to go to the Fourth of July parade in town. The walk from our house was short, only four blocks, but still way too long for me and for my grandfather, too. Rick drove us, and my mom and sisters followed with Izzy.

When they caught up with us, I noticed how slowly Izzy was walking. She lay down and didn't move throughout the whole noisy parade. Even when the fire trucks blew their horns, she didn't twitch.

An elderly man bent down to pat her head and

said, "Poor ol' dog!" Curious, he asked, "How old is she?"

When I told him she was only four, I don't think he believed me. All throughout the parade, people glanced at Izzy, and their comments drifted back to me. "Poor ol' hound dog!"

She's not old! I thought. She's only four! Yes, she has a liver shunt, but she's doing well, much better than her vets expected! I got really worried when Mom said, "She does seem to be struggling with the short walk, Gabe. Maybe you should take her to see Dr. Sandy and have her liver checked. I hope she's fine, but things could be getting worse. It's a miracle she has done as well as she has."

A sick feeling welled up in my stomach.

I called to make an appointment with the vet, but Mom took Izzy in for the visit by herself. I had been up all night, sick with worry, and my stomach was too upset for me to go anywhere.

The test results came back. Izzy's liver was all right—better than it had been, in fact, before she'd been diagnosed with her shunt.

But the vet had noticed something else. She'd told Mom that Izzy looked just like me.

Mom laughed. "Yes, Gabe and Izzy are both kind of floppy," she agreed.

The vet didn't laugh. She just said it again. "Izzy moves just like Gabe."

"Don't tell me dogs get muscle disease!" Mom exclaimed.

"I'm sorry, Rhonda," the vet answered. "It is very rare, but they do."

Izzy needed more tests. And the news wasn't good. Izzy did have a rare type of muscle disease. I never did learn the name; I didn't want to know. All I needed to know was how to take care of her. It turned out there wasn't much I could do except keep Izzy as comfortable as possible.

One of Izzy's vets once told a reporter who was doing a story about us, "I've been a vet for a long time, but I've never seen anything like this before. Gabe and Izzy are so bonded."

She sure was right about that.

And Izzy's new diagnosis bonded us even more. Our diseases were not the same, but our symptoms were almost identical. I stumbled, Izzy stumbled. My muscles were weak; so were Izzy's. We were both wobbly; it was hard for us to balance. I had wheels (my wheelchair), and Izzy did, too (she traveled in a wagon when she had to get somewhere beyond a short walk). Our diseases were both progressive and we both hated going to the doctor!

Stairs were as tough for Izzy as they were for me. I scooted up and down the stairs on my butt to my bedroom and to do my laundry. Izzy got her two front paws on one step and then her back paws, one at a time, up on that same step. Then she started again. It took us awhile, but we never gave up! When we were outside, we both used the wheelchair ramp that my papa had built, knowing that one day I would have no choice but to give in. It was easier and quicker.

When it comes to Izzy and me, there are more coincidences than anyone can explain. As I've said before, her registered name, "Building a Mystery," really says it all. Her presence in my life is a mystery, a beautiful and astonishing one.

A vet once told me that she believes dogs will sometimes take on their owner's conditions as part of their caregiving nature.

How else could it be that this dog, my dog, is so close to me in so many ways? How could she have found me just when I needed her so much? Did it all just happen randomly? I don't think so. I don't think that the coincidences connecting Izzy and me are coincidences at all. There is no doubt in my mind that Izzy and I were meant to be together.

Chapter Twelve

FALLING

Since I'd been taking care of Izzy and speaking in schools, I'd gotten more comfortable using a wheelchair. Still, I didn't like the thought of using one every day. I'd get in my chair to go on a trip or visit Izzy's vet, but at home I'd still try to stay on my feet. It didn't always work. I fell a lot.

Bruises. A cut lip. Torn ligaments in my ankle. A broken nose. Slipping on the step, tumbling to the bottom, I hurt myself over and over, but I'd still get up. Mom wanted me to use a walker, and even went so far as having one shipped to the house, but I refused to use it. I'd rather crawl.

Using the wheelchair at home meant I'd really be accepting defeat. I'd never walk, run, or dance again. That wasn't something I was ready to admit—until one summer day when I was sitting at the kitchen table.

Mom and Rick were at work. Madeline, ten years old, was upstairs, singing along with a song she loved. She would always close her door and think no one could hear her, but the rest of us would sit in the living room and laugh. How adorable she was, singing her heart out.

My stomach was growling. I decided to make myself an instant breakfast drink. I grabbed onto the tall, heavy table that Mom and Rick had gotten especially for me, to make it easier for me to get around, and wobbled around the kitchen.

I'd just poured the powder into my favorite Goofy mug when I lost my balance. I started to fall backward. I tried to grab the sink, but it was wet and slippery and I couldn't hold on. When I hit the floor, I was on my left side with my arm trapped underneath my body.

At once my arm began to burn like it was on fire. It hurt so much I could hardly catch my breath. My face was pressed against the floor.

When I called out to Madeline, my voice was just a whisper.

I tried again and again, but Madeline couldn't hear me over the music.

At last my grandfather heard me from his apartment in our basement and came hurrying up. He wanted to lift me, but I told him firmly not to touch me.

"Don't touch me!" was something my family was used to hearing from me. When I'd fall, I'd get so frustrated with my own body that I would snap at anyone who tried to help me back up, telling them that I was fine and I could do it. But this was different. The pain was excruciating, and I knew there was something seriously wrong. If Papa moved me, he might cause more damage and more pain.

I was on fire, and began gasping for air.

Papa yelled for Madeline, and she raced down the stairs. As soon as she saw me, she grabbed the phone to call Mom.

I was starting to pass out, but I could hear Madeline on the phone. "Mom, Gabe wants you to come home." She paused, so Mom must have been talking. "Gabe fell," Madeline said.

Mom was used to me falling. She didn't want to leave work unless it was a real emergency, so she had Madeline ask me, "Do you want Mom to call 911?"

"No," I managed to say. I was pretty sure I was badly hurt, but calling an ambulance felt a lot like admitting defeat. My body had let me down once again, but maybe I could overcome it, the way I always had. Maybe I could get back on my feet just one more time. But Mom heard me crying in the background. She knew she had to come home.

"Gabe," Madeline said, "Mom will be right here."

Madeline got me a pillow and put one under my head and Papa carefully rolled me over so I could breathe better.

It wasn't long before paramedics were standing over me, cutting off my shirt. I kept blacking out. Caitlin got home before they lifted me into the ambulance, and then Mom arrived. She had been praying the entire way.

I'd severely broken one bone, dislocated another in my elbow, and damaged a nerve. While I lay on a gurney at the hospital, waiting for my doctor to look at the X-rays, Mom stood near me with tears in her eyes. I looked up at her and told her, "Don't feel sorry for me. I did it my way. I wasn't going down until I was taken down!"

It took a permanent plate and six screws to repair my broken bones. And after that—no more avoiding the wheelchair. I had to admit that I needed it, even at home.

It seemed to take forever for my arm to stop hurting. Night after night and day after day my arm ached. I hated to take medication for the pain, so I suffered it out. I remember asking Mom if my arm would ever feel better, and she said she believed it would heal.

Although I was in pain, I had schools to visit. I didn't want to let anybody down, even with my arm in a cast. In the end, I only had to reschedule one school.

I tried not to let anyone see how much my arm was hurting. I'd come too far to stop now. Giving up wasn't an option; that was how my mother, my grandmother (Mima), and my grandfather (Papa) had lived their lives, and I wasn't about to be any different, now that Izzy had made my world better.

And my mom was right. My arm slowly healed. I could get back to my life, telling people about Izzy, and about me.

Chapter Thirteen

TODAY

My mom returned from work one Thursday night and settled down on the sofa to watch TV. I spoke up, keeping my voice casual, and told her that the *Today* show had called.

She laughed. "Yeah, right, Gabe! I'm not falling for another one of your tricks."

Rick and I both tease Mom something fierce. And we're always playing jokes on her. I kept my face straight. "Go check the message yourself."

"I am not getting up," Mom answered. "I'm not that gullible, Gabe. I've had a really busy day and need to rest right now."

Rick finally decided to find out if I was serious

or not. He got up off the sofa and pushed the play button on the answering machine. "She's not kidding, Rhonda Kay," he told my mom. "They really did call and want you to call them ASAP."

Mom couldn't believe it, but it was true. She called back the next day, Friday. On Tuesday a crew from the *Today* show stood in our living room. It was the day after my birthday.

There were interviews at home, and then the crew followed me to a high school where they filmed me speaking to a gym full of kids. Then it was time to come home for more interviews. I'll never forget how comfortable the interviewer, Jenna Wolfe, made me feel. There's one particular question she asked that has always stayed with me. Did I have a favorite quote?

The one I shared with her, by the poet Heather Darling-Cortes, has meant a lot to me for some time.

To the world you may be just one person,
But to one person you may be the world.

I'll never forget the way Jenna lit up as she smiled. I think she saw and understood just what that quote means to me.

The *Today* show aired my segment on Good Friday. Even before it was finished, e-mails asking if I could come and speak were arriving through my Web site. I've spoken at schools, conferences, youth groups, a Rotary Club, and the International Reading Association Convention in Phoenix, Arizona. Twelve hundred people came to hear me speak there, a reminder that I've come a long way from talking to a class or two of children in an elementary school—and feeling nervous about that. By now audiences of up to three thousand students have heard the message Izzy and I have to share, and I've appeared in numerous magazines including *AKC Family Dog, Guideposts, Cosmopolitan,* and *Woman's World.* Izzy and I were also featured in a *National Geographic* book about dogs.

People call me a celebrity all the time. But I tell them, "I am not the celebrity; my dog Izzy is. I am just Gabe, a voice for the bullied." I never set out to be an extraordinary speaker; I just tell the truth about what school was like for me. And students hear me. They feel a real connection with me, because I've been through the things that too many of them experience.

But everything that I'm able to accomplish is due to Izzy. Without Izzy, I would never have become the voice that our nation's schools need.

Being interviewed for the *Today* show made me realize how much I had changed. It wasn't so long ago that I was afraid to leave home in case I saw or met the people who had bullied me in school. I was afraid to meet strangers, afraid to answer questions, afraid to have a picture taken of me in my wheelchair.

My love for Izzy changed all that. Now I've had cameras pointed right at me and millions are seeing the photos. I am not ashamed of being seen or heard.

Izzy came to me at a time when I desperately needed a friend—a friend who would love me no matter what. And it is Izzy's presence at assemblies that is often the key to unlocking the hearts of the students who hear me. They can accept the message I have to spread: unlike my disease, bullying is a choice.

I didn't have a choice about many of the things that happened to me in my life and neither did Izzy. I didn't have a choice about losing my sense of balance and the ability to walk and to dance.

Izzy didn't have a choice about her health issues or her inability to walk. But I do have a choice about treating people decently. Everybody has that choice. You have a choice today, either to be a bully or not be a bully. Who are you going to be? Someone who bullies, someone who stands by, or someone who takes a stand against bullying?

I love seeing posters that read: "Izzy says, 'No School Bullying.'" Izzy really does have a voice. Her unconditional love is something she offers to everyone she meets. I am often told it speaks volumes.

If someone had asked me, several years back, what I would be doing with my life after high school, not in my wildest dreams would I have imagined that I'd be up on a stage, speaking out in public. Especially not about bullying. But that's where I am—where Izzy brought me.

I'll never be a prima ballerina. But I am still dancing. I am on a new stage, dancing a new dance, making the world a better place—one school at a time.

CONCLUSION

I know many of you saw my story on Animal Planet or have seen stories about Izzy and me in magazines or newspapers. Perhaps Izzy and I have even spoken at your school. Please don't be sad, but Izzy has passed away. She was not expected to live past a year, but she lived to be nine and a half. She traveled to schools with me for seven and a half years and never missed an assembly. I say Izzy had perfect attendance!

I never wanted to lose my daughter, my Izzy girl. It was my dream that she would live forever. And I think she will in fact live on in the minds and hearts of students, educators, and others who have been touched by hearing about us. So in that way, my dream has come true.

It has also come true in another way.

I have a new furry girl, born on December 12, 2012. Her name is ILO, and it stands for Izzy Lives On.

Izzy was an extraordinary dog. Mom called her Angel Izzy, because she breathed life back into me. Instead of hiding in my room, ashamed of myself, I played with Izzy, bought her the things she needed, took her to appointments at the vet's. Because of my dog, I once more became a part of the world.

Izzy changed other lives as well. When she developed a disease very similar to mine, she landed us on TV and launched us into becoming voices for bullied students all over the world. A lot of students have health issues, a lot of students have been bullied, but there was only one Izzy dog! It was Izzy who made our message stand out.

Izzy loved going to schools and meeting students. She knew she would get lots of belly rubs! Thousands of students rubbed her soft, warm tummy. She knew she was loved. And she knew when it was time to go.

Izzy let me know when it was her last assembly. Lying slightly in front of me, she lifted her head and gazed into my eyes. She almost never did this, since she couldn't hold her head up long. I knew she was telling me that it was time for her to leave. Her mission here was accomplished.

On May 18, 2009, Izzy passed away.

She had done wonderful things on this earth; she had given me the gift of strength to go on with my life without constant fear. She had made me whole, healed my broken spirit, and given me self-confidence. Because of her, I could make something positive out of my negative school days. I could take all of the bullying I'd lived through and turn it around, using that pain to enlighten students and save thousands of them from enduring what I had endured.

I had taken care of Izzy for nine and a half years, watching her lie beside my wheelchair at schools, conferences, and restaurants, and on airplanes. My life would be so different without her! When I gave my first assembly without Izzy by my side, I burst into tears. I felt horrible for students who would never meet her. I hated to disappoint them. Could my message go on without Izzy?

Amazingly, the answer was yes. I began to notice students were listening to me even more intently when Izzy was no longer there. You could hear a pin drop. How could that be? I realized that students connected with me because they, too, had lost their loved pets. It drew us even closer together, and they listened to my anti-bullying message with new understanding and sympathy.

Mom said she would get me another coonhound if I wanted, but how could I? My heart was still broken. I didn't want another dog; the very idea made me feel guilty. I worried about what Izzy would think. I didn't want her to feel I had replaced her. How could my angel ever be replaced?

I sat onstage alone. Who could fill Izzy's shoes?

Bob Urban, the owner of Izzy's mother, Faye, let my family borrow Izzy's cousin Dinah. Dinah was a sweet girl, and I agreed to take her along so students could get an idea of what Izzy had looked like.

Dinah was three when she came to live with us. I loved her very much, and the students loved her as well, but I didn't have the bond with her I'd had with Izzy. How could I? She was a full-grown dog when she came to my home, not a little puppy who needed me night and day. And she was a family dog, not all mine, as Izzy had been.

After three years of traveling and accompanying me to speaking events, Dinah was diagnosed with jawbone cancer and passed away. She was loved and missed, too. Who would help carry on Izzy's message now?

I began to take my sisters' dogs with me: Dominic, Buckeye, Lindsey Belle. After all, they had been Izzy's friends, and I loved them, too. I even took Poo Poo, a rescue dog who belonged to my stepdad, Rick. Poo Poo had a broken tail, and no one wanted him until Rick brought him home. Students loved all of them, but it wasn't the same as having a coonhound. I missed being with a long-eared companion. I missed the chance to show students what Izzy had looked like.

I began to feel a yearning inside me. The desire for my own puppy slowly filled my head. I told my mom, "One day I will get another dog like Izzy."

She seemed surprised. It was the first time in years she'd heard words like this from me. I was surprised myself.

Whenever the topic of another pet came up, my mom would say, "No more dogs!" But this time she said something else. "Maybe one day," my mom answered me. "When we move where we have a bigger yard."

But later my mom told me she knew the timing was right.

I was invited to go to the Eukanuba Dog Show in Orlando, Florida, and saw the black and tan coonhounds (and many other breeds, too). My heart began to beat fast when I saw the familiar black and brown coats, the long ears, the sad eyes. "I want a puppy," I told my mom again. I like all dogs, but I am in love with coonhounds. There is something so sweet and unique about them. I knew one day I would have another.

Little did I know that Mom and my stepdad Rick, Bob Urban, and Chris Hooker, owner of Izzy's dad, Bruce, had begun planning a surprise. At the dog show Bob showed Mom a picture of ILO. My new puppy had already been born and I had no idea!

My sister Madeline, who was finishing high school back in Michigan, was in on the surprise. For Valentine's Day, she told me she'd mailed a package, and it should get to me on or before February 14. After that she called every day, asking if her package had arrived. I wanted to know what it would be, but she wouldn't tell me. "Is it a big box or small box?" I demanded. She laughed and told me it was big and heavy. She loves to tease and goof around, so she might have mailed me anything. She knows how much I adore DOTS and Hershey bars with almonds. Could it be a huge box full of them?

I love getting packages. I ordered all of Izzy's toys through the mail. So I looked forward to Madeline's package, too. I could not imagine what she'd sent me! Never in my wildest dreams did I ever think it would be a puppy named ILO—short for Izzy Lives On.

The truth was that my Valentine's Day surprise wasn't from Madeline—she was just trying to increase my anticipation and excitement. In fact my present was from Bob Urban, and it arrived at the Orlando International Airport. My mom and Rick told me they were going to help my sister Caitlin with her car, but really they went to pick up my brand-new puppy.

Mom tucked ILO snugly in a box wrapped in pink patterned paper. The box also had a baby blanket with pink hearts for ILO to snuggle on, a pink collar, a leash, and a card bigger than the puppy herself.

When Mom and Rick got home, Mom walked

in and told me that the UPS driver had left a big box by the front door for me. She went back out and brought it inside.

Would it be candy? Chocolate? Something I'd love?

Yes, it would.

A soft, silky, adorable coonhound puppy jumped right out of the box. I was speechless!

Just like it had been with Izzy, it was love at first sight. ILO looked like my dear girl Izzy, and I was to be her new mommy. At first I called her baby Izzy.

I opened up the card that had come with her. Inside was written, "YOU AND ME WERE MEANT TO BE."

ILO is perfect! I can't wait until I take her to my upcoming speaking engagements. I know students and adults will fall in love with her.

With Izzy by my side, it was amazing to see how students opened up to me. They let my anti-bullying message into their hearts. The thousands of letters that are mailed or posts written on my online guestbook are evidence: I was given a gift to connect with students and to bring about positive change. Izzy brought that gift to life, and I know that ILO will do the same.

Not all students understand bullying. They're told not to do it, that it's wrong, that it's not acceptable. But it's sometimes hard for those words to sink in.

When the human heart is touched, and students feel what bullying has done to one person's life, they understand the anti-bullying message in a way they haven't before. When students *feel* it, they *get* it! They understand and decide to change their hurtful behavior.

Izzy will never truly die as long as she stays in the hearts of the students who have met her or heard about her. When they take the Gabe and Izzy Anti-bullying Pledge, they are keeping her memory alive. And ILO will do the same. Her name says it all: Izzy Lives On! My new little girl will do just what Izzy always did—use her loving and caring nature to change the lives of those who are lucky enough to know her.

ILO sits under my wheelchair, follows me, and cuddles with me so sweetly. She runs beside me when I ride my recumbent bike. I recently noticed that the little brown patch under her tail is in the shape of a heart. Yes, just like Izzy, ILO and me— we were meant to be.

Pet Passings

SARAH IZABEL "IZZY" FORD

was born on New Year's Eve 1999 (12/31/1999) in Sanford, NC. Her parents were Bruce and Faye, two Black & Tan Coonhounds. She was the runt in a litter of 5; her sib-

lings are Ben, Dan, Alice and Grace. The puppies in the litter were identified by colored collars, before she was named Izzy she was known as "the pink girl" and later as "Itty Bitty" because of her size. The litter was cared for by Chris & Terry Hooker, a Bassett hound named Festus and many others. When she arrived in Gabrielle "Gabe" Ford's life, her adoption mom, she was given the name Sarah Izabel "Izzy" Ford. Her new litter mates were Rick, Rhonda, Caitlin and Madeline. Before Gabe received her dog, she was told by her mom Rhonda, she would have to be responsible for her in every way, since it was Gabe's dog. When Izzy was about 5 months old she was diagnosed with portal systemic shunt, a life threatening liver disease. Since Gabe was responsible for her care, she had to go to the vet's office and talk with them. This forced Gabe out of her house. After years of being bullied and abused in high school, Gabe resorted to hiding in her house and refrained from going in public. Izzy's illness slowly drew Gabe out of her home. After generous donations from local and distant patrons and veterinarians, Izzy got the help she needed. The vets helping Izzy didn't expect her to live past 1 year. Since she has surpassed that life expectancy, they called her "a miracle." An article that was written about Izzy and Gabe's fight to help save her caught the attention of Animal Planet, the national television channel. Their story "Izzy & Gabe" aired on the segment A Pet Story. It was aired over 68 times within 4 years and became the viewers favorite 'A Pet Story.' A comment made in that show helped launch Gabe into speaking out about bullying all around the nation in school, etc. Three years after 'A Pet Story' Izzy was diagnosed with a rare form of muscular dystrophy. This diagnosis was very similar to Gabe's childhood diagnoses of Friedreich's ataxia, a rare form of neuromuscular disease. The new diagnosis brought Gabe out into the public once again. Since then Gabe & Izzy's story has been chronicled in Jerry Lewis's MDA Quest magazine, which the duo is featured on the front cover. They've also been in the AKC's Family Dog and Gazette, the world wide magazines Cosmopolitan and Guidepost, several newspaper articles, television and radio interviews, the Today show which aired in March '08 and is currently viewable at www.gabeanddizzy.com. Gabe & Izzy's life story and journey together will be released as a memoir called 'Still Dancing' due out in June. Izzy was 9½ years old and her muscular dystrophy had progressed beyond manageable help. She was put to rest on Monday, May 18th, 2009. Izzy has touched hundreds of thousands of lives around the world with her story and long velvety ears. I want to thank the myriad of students for their thoughts and prayers. Over the years Gabe and her family acquired 3 more canine family members, Dominic, LindseyBelle and recently Jack Sparrow. The two feline members are Bob and Sweetie. They all have been part of her livelihood. Izzy's legendary life and her 'No School Bullying/Anti Violence" message will continue to live on and help others.

154

TO KIDS, PARENTS, AND EDUCATORS

You have a choice today. You can choose to listen to the message in this book, or you can choose not to. If you choose to hear, and think about, and accept what you have read, then you can choose whether or not you are going to apply this message to your life. You can choose whether you will keep thinking about what you have read here as you go through school, and into your adult life, and even when you raise the children you may one day have.

Listening to the message of this book is a choice. Just like bullying is a choice. Bullying is something done on purpose.

The good news is that, since bullying is a choice, it can also be stopped.

If we are honest with ourselves, we'll admit that at some time in our lives we, too, have bullied someone. Or have watched someone being bullied and done nothing about it. But even if those things happened yesterday, that doesn't mean they have to happen again tomorrow. We can all choose to change our behavior for the better, anytime we want.

We live in an imperfect world. There will always be bullying, but together we can prevent a lot of it, if we choose not to ignore it. We can create a world where all kids can grow into healthy, secure adults.

Are we willing to try to make the world a better place?

TO THOSE WHO'VE BULLIED OTHERS

Bullying means being cruel to someone who is weaker than you are. Bullying is more than pushing or hitting. You might not think of yourself as a bully. But have you ever called someone a name? Made fun of someone who was different?

Many students don't realize they are bullies

because they have never thought of themselves that way. They just think they're "messing around." Having fun. But it's anything but fun for the person who's the target.

Have you ever . . .

. . . pushed or shoved someone?

. . . shut someone out? Refused to sit on the bus or at a lunch table with someone?

. . . labeled someone by calling them a particular name?

. . . criticized the way someone dressed or looked?

. . . spread a rumor about someone you didn't like?

. . . asked someone else to tease or push someone?

. . . posted a negative comment on a blog or Web site about someone else?

. . . treated someone in a way you wouldn't want to be treated yourself?

. . . sent a mean e-mail, text, or instant message?

If you answered yes to any of these questions, then you're just one of many people who might not even realize that their behavior hurts others.

Many kids bully others because it makes them feel powerful. Or they might see something they want—money, jewelry, whatever—and take it from a weaker person. Maybe they're acting out problems at home, or copying something done by a classmate they admire. Some need attention. Others may need to feel in control by winning at everything they do.

A person who bullies is a person who needs to dominate others. For whatever reason.

If any of this sounds familiar, you need to look inside. Ask yourself, "Why am I acting this way?"

Think about what your actions will do to others. How do you want to be remembered later in life? When you're attending your high school reunion, what do you want people to think about you? Are you doing things now that you'll regret? Why live with those regrets when you don't have to?

I didn't have a choice about the disease that took away my ability to walk, run, and dance. But you *do* have a choice about how you treat others. Each day you can decide what kind of a person you will be. Will you bring more pain into the world? Or less? Will you make someone's day, or break someone's day?

Instead of bullying, look for positive ways to interact. Offer a compliment. Ask a question. Make a joke that doesn't have a mean punch line. Try to be kind when you see people who are different.

If you've been cruel to someone, apologize. I can't begin to tell you how many students told me how freeing it is to simply say "I'm sorry." They feel good. They know that bullying is over for them.

It can be for you, too.

You have a choice.

Posted by Heather

You came to my school and everyone loved your speech. You have made a big difference in my life. I get very frustrated with people very easily and I take stuff out on other people because of problems at home. I know I should not, but it just happens. A lot of kids made fun of other people and it's not right. I am starting to realize that it does hurt other people's feelings and I stopped after your speech.

Posted by Kevin

I really loved your talk. . . . I really enjoyed it and I hope everyone else did. I wish that I could help make your dreams come true, but I know that it can't be changed or get better. I also learned a lot from your talk. I like fooling around with kids like the way you got bullied.

When you talked about it I felt bad and I said sorry to a lot of those kids to whom I'd been mean, and I never knew that it was bullying. Now that you have taught me all that good stuff I am going to stop doing what I did to bully kids.

TO THE WITNESS

If you're not being bullied, you still have a responsibility to those who are. Don't keep silent because you want to protect yourself, or because you think it might win you points with a more popular crowd. A school is a community. Do you want to live in a community where people get hurt every day? Dig deep inside yourself and ask, "Do I want people treated like this in my school? Would I like my friends or my little sister to be shoved or snickered at or called names? Would it be okay if someone treated *me* like that?"

Support the victim. Don't laugh at a bully's actions. Don't make the victim feel worse than he or she already does. If nobody laughs or chimes in, bullies will feel weak.

Sometimes the best way to stop a bully is to reach out to the victim. Bullies target people who are alone. Your presence can make a victim safer. If you see kids who are always alone, go to them. Walk with them from the bus. Sit with them at lunch. Choose those people when you pick a team in gym or class.

Children who are teased dread coming to school. You might make that dread go away. You might even learn a little bit about those people and why they are different.

Find the strength to reach out to a parent or a teacher or another adult if you see bullying. This isn't tattling or "telling" on someone. It's making sure your school is safe. Sometimes a bully's victim is too afraid or embarrassed to seek help. You may be able to get that person the help he or she is too frightened to ask for.

Not everyone is going to be your cup of tea. You don't have to be best friends with every person who's being picked on. But you don't have to stand back and watch someone make fun of them, either.

You have a choice.

Posted by Alyssa

I hope you have fun going all around the world to schools to talk about bullying! P.S. I made a new friend because she was being bullied and playing by herself. She is so nice.

Everybody is responsible for his or her actions. And the victim has two important responsibilities as well. The first is to seek help and not give up until you find someone who can make things better. The second is to forgive.

I told you about "Jason"—the boy who punched me, day after day. He stopped hitting me when he understood what it was doing to me. My willingness to forgive him helped me to go on.

I have forgiven those who bullied me, and I tell students they should do the same, even if the person who hurt them never apologizes. Forgiving someone will help you release the anger and the bitterness that could otherwise destroy you. Forgiveness is healing. When you forgive, it actually helps you more than the person being forgiven. It means you are no longer letting the people who hurt you be in control of your thoughts and emotions. You are taking away some of the bully's power over you.

People who are cruel need help. Many times bullies were once bullied themselves. You'd thinking that nobody who'd been a bully's victim would be cruel to another person, but that isn't always the case. Maybe the bully is insecure. Maybe he just wants attention.

Maybe she wants to change but just doesn't know how.

When you're willing to tell a bully how you feel, that bully has a chance to change. Bullies won't always take that chance. But some may. Jason did.

Speak up. Forgive.

You have a choice.

ARE YOU BEING BULLIED?

What to Do (and What Not to Do)

Getting bullied? You might feel helpless, but you don't need to. There's hope. Use your voice. Ask for help. You can stop the bullying and improve your life.

- Do reach out to someone. Find teachers, educators, or parents you trust and tell them what has been happening to you. If the first person you tell doesn't help you, ask another.
- Don't think the bullying will just go away.
- Do join extracurricular activities or clubs with kids you enjoy. You shouldn't let the bully take the fun out of your life.
- Don't avoid the world. Don't skip school or stay out of classes. Don't let those bullies take your education, too!
- Do stand up for yourself, if you feel safe. Bullies thrive on fear. Ask them to stop their behavior. Be

confident. What they're doing is wrong, and on some level they know it.

- Don't bully back. Don't push or shove or call names. Be above that bully's behavior.
- Do remember that it's not your fault you are being bullied.
- Don't hurt yourself. You might become sad or depressed and want to hurt yourself because you think there's no other answer, but there is. Go to an adult and find help.

TO PARENTS

Parents can set standards of behavior that their children should follow, in and out of school. Encourage your child to help others. If they witness bullying, they should speak up and get help. Teach your children to respect differences. Share stories from your own childhood. These stories will come alive in the minds and hearts of your kids, and will be examples from which they can learn.

If a child accuses your own child of bullying, listen. Don't dismiss what happened as "roughhousing" or say "Kids will be kids." Even good children can make bad choices. If a student or an educator comes to you with a bullying concern, that person is not telling you that your child is awful or that you are an awful parent. Actually, that person is giving both you and your child a chance to show how good you can be. Listen to the situation. Correct behavior you don't approve of. Show your child you take these issues seriously, and that will help him or her change.

If you suspect that your child is being bullied, encourage him or her to tell you so that you can reach out to others. Talk to educators and to the other child's parents. Your child needs to feel comfortable coming to you with problems, and needs to see that telling you really will make a difference.

Posted by Tyler

The day you guys came and had the assembly, I told my parents that people were bullying me. They did something about it. You gave me courage.

Parents, think about your own behavior as well. How do you react to people from different social, economic, or racial backgrounds? Do you tell jokes to your friends that you think your child can't hear? He or she probably can and does hear—if not what you say, then the attitude behind it. When you ridicule a person or a group for being different, you teach your child that ridicule is acceptable.

If you see TV shows or movies that mock people who are different, then you can use these as opportunities to teach your child acceptance. If does not matter if we are short, tall, thin, overweight, or scarred. A person's skin color or hair texture doesn't matter. Religion or ethnicity doesn't matter. Physical or mental disability doesn't matter. Not when it comes to being treated decently.

We need to learn to be more accepting of other people's differences. Think about it: if we were all the same, wouldn't it be a really boring world?

That is something you can teach your child.

You have a choice.

ARE YOUR CHILDREN BEING BULLIED?

Not all parents realize that their children are being bullied. Some children feel embarrassed about telling anyone about the teasing or the tormenting they've endured. The love you feel toward your child can even make it hard for you to see that he or she might be disliked or treated unfairly. Look for the following signs:

Does your child . . .

. . . ask to stay home when he or she isn't sick?

. . . ask to be excused from certain classes?

. . . act withdrawn or quiet?

. . . avoid areas where other children might be—bus stops, school events, extracurricular activities?

If you see any of these signs in your child, act quickly. Talk to your child alone and make him or her feel as comfortable as possible. Mention that you've noticed some changes and you'd like to talk about them. Make sure your child feels safe opening up to you. If he or she isn't ready to talk, remain open to hearing more another day.

TO EDUCATORS

There are many reasons educators must take action against bullying. Look at the recent incidents of school violence. Often it is the victims of bullying who are frustrated enough to turn to revenge. In addition, children who are repeatedly bullied are at greater risk of committing suicide. They feel hopeless and see death as their only means of escape.

Bullying is one of the most underrated and enduring problems in schools today. Schools are a prime location for bullies to thrive.

I urge schools to foster an anti-bullying culture. Often this starts with education for students and educators. Many curriculums are available for schools willing to give their teachers and counselors the tools they need. Presentations like mine can help students who need to change their behavior. But you still need to be vigilant after the assemblies end to ensure that every child is being treated with respect.

We must address bullying in every classroom. It's not acceptable, and all educators are responsible for assuring that all schools foster a safe environment where students can learn. Addressing bullying is your choice!

FOR PARENTS AND EDUCATORS: HOW TO HELP

Adults who see children struggling with bullying are often at a loss about how to help. Take a look at these tips from the U.S. Department of Health and Human Services on their Web site StopBullying.gov.

• Stop bullying as it is happening.

Separate the kids involved.

Get the help of another adult if you need it.

Don't ignore the bullying or think, The kids can work it out themselves.

- Find out what happened.
   - Don't try to sort out all the facts right on the spot.
   - Talk to each kid involved separately.
   - Get the story from several sides, including bystanders or witnesses.
   - Listen to everybody without blaming.
- Support the child who was bullied.
   - Listen.
   - Assure that the bullying was not his or her fault.
   - Give advice about what to do if the situation happens again.
- Support the child who bullied.
   - Make sure the child knows what the problem behavior was.
   - Show the child that bullying is taken seriously.
   - Work with the child to make amends.
   - For more details on how to stop bullying, visit StopBullying.gov.

RESOURCES

Change starts with education. Take a look at these Web sites to learn more about me, bullying awareness, and Friedreich's ataxia.

GABE AND IZZY

www.gabeandizzy.com
Learn more about Gabe's anti-bullying campaign and find out where she's speaking next. Leave a message on her online guestbook, book her for your own group or school, or make a donation to the Friends of Gabe & Izzy Charity.

BULLYING

Center for the Study and Prevention of Violence
http://www.colorado.edu/cspv/resources
A clearinghouse of information for educators, parents, and students on school violence and bullying.

Make Time to Listen, Take Time to Talk
http://store.samhsa.gov/product/15-Make-Time-To-Listen-Take-Time-To-Talk-About-Bullying/SMA08-4321
Provided by the Department of Substance Abuse and Mental Health Services Administration, this campaign is based on the idea that parents who talk with their children for at least fifteen minutes a day are better able to help those children build positive relationships. The site offers free publications on dealing with and preventing bullying for parents, educators, caregivers, teens, and children.

Stop Bullying
http://www.stopbullying.gov
This Web site from the U.S. Department of Health and Human Services offers tips on identifying and dealing with bullying for victims, bystanders, educators, and parents.

FRIEDREICH'S ATAXIA

Friedreich's Ataxia Research Alliance (FARA)

www.CureFA.org

This national nonprofit seeks to cure Friedreich's ataxia through research. Look to this site for results from any new studies and trials.

National Ataxia Foundation (NAF)

www.ataxia.org

This nonprofit improves the lives of those impacted by FA through support, education, and research. This site provides links to support groups, events, research, and chat rooms.

Muscular Dystrophy Association (MDA)

mda.org

This nonprofit health agency aims to cure muscular dystrophy, ALS, and related diseases through funding and worldwide research. Look to this site for fact sheets on different kinds of neuromuscular diseases, to find clinics or support groups near you, and to connect with other families.

AMERICAN BLACK AND TAN COONHOUND CLUB

abtcc.com

Provides information for owners of black and tan coonhounds—Izzy's breed.

ACKNOWLEDGMENTS

The book would not have been possible without Bob Urban and Chris Hooker, Izzy's breeders. Thank you for your part in fulfilling my dream of owning a female coonhound with extra long ears. Because of you I met my special furry girl, Izzy. I am also grateful to Dr. Sandy Smith and her staff at Animal Health Clinic. You cared for Izzy as if she were your own. You're the best.

I send a huge hug to the citizens of Fenton, Michigan, for their love and support. Saving my dog's life was my heart's cry, and you responded valiantly. You understood Izzy's impact on my life and donated funds to help pay her extensive medical bills. I will never forget your kindness. A very special thanks goes out to the Fenton Chamber of Commerce.

Thank you also to the Family Doctor's Clinic, Dr. E. J. Daros and his wife, Jackie Daros, Dr. Anthony Daros, and Dr. Darla Murphy. You've always been there for my family. You're all very special to me.

Thanks to Barb LaPointe, Pat Schleh, Sandy Matthee, Nancy Rowe, Margie Bergren, Jane Rauch, Janelle Dowdle, Jacket Acs, Shelly Coad, Kelly Burgess, Roger Davis, Laura Ouellette, Debbie Wheeler, Shelia Smith, Becky Bugala, Davette Shelton, Marcie Carpenter, Barb Warden, John Spencer, Kace Wekem, Cathy and Dave Ehred, Steve and Emily Curiak, Rosie Fitzgerald, Jennifer Turner, and the Freedom Center and Cornerstone Church friends who brought meals to my family to save my mom from cooking during busy times.

My dear friend Amanda, you and your family have given me a treasure chest of wonderful memories. I was privileged to be your maid of honor and then to have your daughter, Allison, born on my birthday—how special!

Sean Nasri, you are a true friend, someone I can talk to and trust. I'm so glad you tracked me down after seeing me on Animal Planet's *A Pet Story*.

Thanks to those Lake Fenton students who had the courage to stand up for me when I was being bullied. Your kindness did not go unnoticed and will never be forgotten.

The students, educators, and friends who have taken the time to write me make my journey worthwhile. The letters and comments have encouraged me and given me strength to continue my work in schools and other places. Knowing my life's journey with Izzy has made a positive difference in the lives of so many has helped me to keep moving toward my goal—teaching the young and others to build a more empathetic society.

To my canine friends, Lindsey Belle and Dominic, and her feline friends Sweetie and Bob: you have always been there to cuddle with me during lonely times. All of you are such a comfort and a huge part of my life.

I send heartfelt thanks to my best friend, Izzy, who I believe had taken on an illness similar to my own as a part of her caregiving nature. I stumbled, and so did Izzy. Izzy's unconditional love propelled me into what I am doing today. She, my hero, gave me wings to fly higher than I could have ever imagined. My heart's desire is that

Izzy will live forever—in the hearts and minds of those touched by her story.

I send special thanks to my family, who have been supportive in so many ways. The sacrifices you've made have not gone unnoticed. Caitlin, Madeline, Aunt Linda, Uncle Bob, Robbie, Tracy, Uncle Steve, and Emily: thanks so much for loving me and always being there.

To Papa, who still lives with us, and Mima, who lives on in our hearts, thanks for your unconditional love. Papa, you're always doing thoughtful things, like making sure my ramp is shoveled so I can get to the car for my events, and waiting in the driveway to help me into the car. Your loving care is a gift. Thanks so much, Papa.

An extra-special thanks to Rick, who wasn't afraid to marry my mom, knowing that I had a disability. He's a very special man who makes me laugh and who has gone out of his way to love me for who I am, never making me feel like a burden. He sees me—not my disability.

Mom, how can I ever thank you enough for your loving support throughout my life? You never gave up on me, calling yourself a blessed woman because God entrusted me to you. The mission Izzy and I took on could not move forward without you. I know how much time you have given up to help me in this endeavor. I will never forget the countless hours you spent driving Izzy and me across the United States to share my story with others. The traffic delays, rain, ice, and snowstorms tried to keep us from reaching our destinations on time, but nothing deters you. Thanks for believing in me and helping to make a difference in the lives of others. Students are opening their hearts, looking beyond my disability, and hearing my message because of you. I love you, Mom. Thank you!

To Eileen Kreit (President and Publisher, Puffin Books): Not everything is just by chance; some things are just meant to be! Meeting you at the International Reading Association Conference was my honor. Had you not cared about the subject of school bullying and taken time to visit with Izzy and me, this book would not be in print. Thanks for believing in us.

Kristin Gilson and the team at Penguin Young Readers Group: You have been mind-blowing to work with! You have consistently considered my thoughts and feelings while working so closely with me to write this book. Some things were painful to share, but you were always so perceptive and helped me handle it all caringly so that it would help others. Isn't that really what life is all about, helping others?

To Torre DeRoche: You are miraculous! Without you I would never have connected with Elizabeth Evans. She is everything you said, down-to-earth (which is a refreshing quality for a NYC literary agent), honest, nurturing, and incredibly talented at what she does. Izzy and I couldn't be in better hands. I will be forever grateful to you.

Elizabeth Evans and team at Jean V. Naggar Literacy Agency Inc.: Thank you, thank you, thank you! These words will never be said or felt enough by my family or me. Elizabeth, you believe as much as we do that Izzy and I have a message to get out to the world. I believe signing you as my agent is definitely another one of those things that was meant to be! You never once waivered. You're the BEST!

Sarah Thompson, thank you for being the type of ghostwriter who is able to get into my head and help me express myself. This is a gift, and I am thankful I chose you and you chose me. I know you are that somebody Izzy and I were meant to link up with. America and abroad will listen and stand up for the bullied because we worked so well together. Much thanks.